HISTORICAL MARKERS

IN

NEW MEXICO

Compiled and Designed by
DEANE G. DELGADO

Edited by
**New Mexico State Records Center
and Archives**

Revised Edition

Ancient City Press
SANTA FE, NEW MEXICO

1990

CONTENTS

International Standard Book Number:
0-941270-62-9 (paperback)
Library of Congress Catalogue Number:
89-081887
Revised Edition
Photo Credits: New Mexico State Parks; U.S. Library of
              Congress; New Mexico Tourism and Travel
              Division; National Park Service, Dept. of
              Interior; New Mexico State Records Center
              and Archives

INTRODUCTION

Welcome to New Mexico, "Land of Enchantment" - the first words to greet travelers as they drive across the borders into this beautiful and historically rich state. These words are also part of the Official Historical Highway Marker program. Historical markers are found throughout New Mexico and "Historical Markers in New Mexico" can help locate these signs and plan trips full of breathtaking scenery and historic sites both old and new.

New Mexico's first efforts to inform the traveling public about this state's great historical background began in 1935. Involved in these efforts were the State Tourist Bureau, the State Highway Commission, the National Park Service, and commercial artist Sostenes Delgado, all of whom contributed to the beginning of the marker program.

Under the present program, the Highway Department, in cooperation with the Travel and Tourism Division, is responsible for all costs relating to the markers. The Highway Department preforms the actual installation and maintenance. The Cultural Properties Review Committee maintains the responsibility for researching and approving the text on all new markers.

Most of the markers are located at turnouts along the state's major highway arterials. However, in the case of the Interstate Highway System, markers are often grouped together at Rest Areas and Ports of entry, as close as possible to the scene of the events being described.

The traveling public has shown an intense interest in these historical markers in New Mexico and many suggestions for potential new sites are made each year. Through the joint efforts of the Travel and Tourism Division, the Highway Department and the Cultural Properties Review Committee, all such suggestions are reviewed on the basis of their merit and practicality, and changes and additions are made in the program as required.

Travelers who have been long accustomed to the distinctive traditional color scheme of the Historical Highway Markers should note that the new markers are printed in white letters on a brown background, in conformity with the federal government's Manual on Uniform Traffic Control Devices Standards. As in the past, most of the markers contain the texts on one side and the "Points of Interest" map plates on the reverse, to help travelers identify sites in the area worthy of a visit.

The editors of these guides would like to acknowledge the contributions of several individuals who have helped to make this edition possible. In the mid-1970's the Cultural Properties Review Committee attempted a large scale systematic revision of the Historical Highway Marker texts. Although never completed or implemented, the work of Myra Ellen Jenkins, Stuart Peckham, Albert Schroeder, Marc Simmons and Spencer Wilson was useful in the formulation of the revised texts. Marker texts for geological or natural historical features were prepared by William O. Hatchell, Kay S. Hatton, and James M. Hill, Bureau of Geology, Department of Energy and Minerals, by Frank E. Kottlowski, Director, Bureau of Mines and Mineral Resources, and by Scott Baldridge, Los Alamos National Laboratories. Peter Green, Planner, State Parks Division, Department of Natural Resources, prepared the texts describing State Parks. The editors would also like to thank the following individuals for their cooperation: E.E. Strahan, Assistant Secretary for Travel and Tourism, John Adams, Senior Program Officer, Tours and Meetings Section, Travel and Tourism Division; Robert Ringer, Traffic Services Section Head, Highway Department, Louis Medrano, former Traffic Services Division Head; Eleanor Mauzy, formerly of the Traffic Services Division; Donald R. Lavash, Historian, State Records Center; Regge Wiseman, Archaeologist, Museum of Indian Arts, Laboratory of Anthropology; Lala O. Baca, Secretary, State Records Center; Russell Davidson, General Library, University of New Mexico; Patrick Beckett, Chairman, and the entire Cultural Properties Review Committee; and Thomas Merlan, Director, and the staff of the Historic Preservation Division, Office of Cultural Affairs; Stanley M. Hordes, Richard Salazar, and Robert Torrez.

New Mexico abounds in natural and historical resources providing many delightful opportunities for sightseeing and relaxation. It is hoped that this volume will serve as a helpful guide for travelers who seek to understand more about the natural and cultural attractions of the state.

A BRIEF HISTORY OF NEW MEXICO

New Mexico is the fifth largest state in the Union. At least eight other states could be neatly fitted into this vast geographic area. Its 121,666 square miles could encompass the combined area of Delaware, Maine, Massachusetts, New Hampshire, New Jersey, New York and Rhode Island.

In population it is comparatively small, ranking 37th in number of inhabitants. However, New Mexico is gaining at a higher rate than the national average, offering many attractions to people wanting to escape the more congested areas of the nation. Consequently, the state is a mixture of many different groups of people who constitute a multi-cultural society. The waves of different people and cultures coming to New Mexico make this state one of the most culturally diverse in the United States.

New Mexico has a unique environment. Life forms (both plant and animal) differ from one place to another. Because of this, scientists have divided the world into seven different areas where some form of life exists. New Mexico contains six of these seven lifezones. The zones are determined by climatic conditions that change, depending on distance from the equator and altitude above sea level. These changes can be seen in plant and animal life as one travels throughout the state.

An outstanding feature of New Mexico is the awesome beauty of the great piney forests. Towering above the wooded land to a height of 13,161 feet is Wheeler Peak located in the upper region of the Sangre de Cristo Mountains. Situated in the southern foothills of the mountains approximately 7,000 feet in elevation is Santa Fe, the capital city. Stable weather conditions help to provide for the mild climate found in this part of the state. Then descending to the sparse, arid area of the plains of the southeast there is so little vegetation that each head of cattle needs eleven acres of grassland to survive. So flat are the prairies of eastern New Mexico that when the pioneers from the east in the nineteenth century crossed the mountains they found almost no landmarks to guide them.

The earliest securely dated remains of man thus far found in what is now New Mexico are called Clovis, after a distinctive style of projectile point, and date to 12,000 years ago. There is a growing body of evidence that these people or their predecessors entered the North American continent from Siberia across the Bering Land Bridge tens of thousands of years ago, but most of that evidence is considered to be circumstantial. These ancient peoples (or Paleoindians), and those who followed (Folsom, Cody, etc.) were largely dependent upon large (now extinct) forms of mammoths, bison, and early forms of camels and horses. This way of life required a semi-nomadic or nomadic existence that allowed the people to anticipate herd movements.

With the retreat of the glaciers, the terrain began drying up, and the lush vegetation withdrew to mountain fastnesses. The lower-lying areas became dominated by plant and animal life accustomed to drier conditions. Out of necessity, man shifted his mode of livelihood to a greater dependence on plant foods supplemented by hunting. A semi-nomadic life-style was still necessary in order to locate and harvest the plant food resources. This new adaptation, called the Archaic, was well established by 5000 B.C. and continued until about the time of Christ or a little later.

During the Archaic period, a new food source, cultivated corn, was introduced from Mexico. Perhaps because of growing population and the increasing competition for plant and animal resources, the native population developed a dependence on corn. As corn became more important in the economy, so too did the need to protect and nurture the young plants. During the first few centuries A.D., most populations in the western two-thirds of New Mexico had begun to settle down in semi-permanent or permanent villages with more substantial forms of houses (called pithouses) and, a little later, began making pottery. These people still relied upon wild plant and animal foods to a great extent, as evidenced by the locations of their villages with easy access to the hinterlands as well as to the farming lands along drainages. The peoples in the eastern third of New Mexico apparently maintained their former semi-nomadic way of life for the next several centuries.

From 500 A.D. onward, New Mexico saw a number of comparatively rapid changes. The peoples throughout the western two-thirds of the state became increasingly restricted to smaller and smaller areas resulting in the development of many regional differences in architecture, ceramics, and other crafts. Housing patterns reflected above-ground forms (pueblos), specialized ceremonial structures (kivas) appeared, ceramic decoration styles evolved quickly, the average size of villages increased, social integration become more complicated, reliance on agriculture intensified, and trade networks were greatly elaborated and expanded. Between 1100 and 1400 A.D., vast areas of New Mexico, including Chaco Canyon, were abandoned by these village dwellers for reasons that are still poorly understood. It seems likely that the reasons varied from locale to locale, but it is probable that all were ultimately triggered in one way or another by subtle climatic shifts that made the rather specialized adaptations of the prehistoric New Mexicans impossible in many regions. These people apparently joined the populations along the Río Grande and in the Ácoma and Zuni regions as well as areas outside of New Mexico. That some of the abandoned areas, including eastern New

Mexico, were still used on occasion by both village agriculturists and by nomadic groups during early Spanish contact period is a matter of record.

Far in advance of any "westward expansion," the first European incursion into New Mexico occurred just a few short decades after the conquest of Mexico in 1519 by Fernando Cortés. Seeking to expand the realms of the king of Spain, Francisco Vásquez de Coronado led an expedition of over 1,000 men and women in 1540 north from Mexico into what is now Arizona, New Mexico, Texas, Oklahoma and Kansas. The Spanish explorers, in search of the mythical, wealthy "Seven Cities of Cíbola," found little in the way of precious metals. But, perhaps more importantly, they uncovered groups of advanced sedentary Indians, whom they labeled "Pueblos," due to the concentration of the native population in *pueblos,* or towns. A combination of severe winters, failure to discover the treasures of Cíbola, and a debilitating injury to Vásquez de Coronado, compelled the Spaniards to return home to Mexico, thus leaving the colonization of New Mexico for another, more permanent enterprise five decades later.

Following the disappointing search for riches of the 1540s, Spanish officials and entrepreneurs turned their attention toward exploiting the lucrative silver mines of northern New Spain closer to the capital of Mexico City. The 1580s and early 90s witnessed several unsuccessful expeditions into New Mexico, including those of Fray Agustín Rodríguez and Francisco Chamuscado (1581), Fray Bernardino Beltrán and Antonio de Espejo (1582), and the unauthorized expeditions of Gaspar Castaño de Sosa (1589), and Francisco Leyva de Bonilla and Antonio Gutíerrez de Humaña (1593). It was not until 1598 that the viceroy of New Spain appointed Juan de Oñate as governor of New Mexico and directed him to settle the area along the upper Río Grande. The viceroy realized that it was necessary at this time to expand the mining frontier, to secure the northern reaches of the viceroyalty against threats by the English, and to Christianize the advanced Indian civilizations in the area. Accompanied by some 200 settlers, including soldiers, families and priests, and over 7000 head of livestock, Oñate headed northward along the Camino Real, and arrived in New Mexico. He established his headquarters first at San Juan, and just months later at San Gabriel at the confluence of the Río Chama and Río Grande. In 1610, the capital was established at the *Villa de Santa Fe,* or Town of Holy Faith, making Santa Fe the oldest capital city in what is now the United States.

New Mexico in the seventeenth century was plagued by isolation, conflicts between civil and ecclesiastical authorities, and extreme demands placed by the Spanish settlers on the native population. The latter situation had deteriorated so badly by 1680, that the Pueblo Indians united under the leadership of Popé to revolt against the Spanish, and they succeeded in driving their conquerors completely out of the province. Under the direction of Diego de Vargas, the Spanish returned to recapture New Mexico in 1693, after 13 years of exile. Vargas and his successors, in an attempt to encourage settlement of the lands in the Río Grande Valley issued land grants for agriculture and grazing to Spanish colonists and reconfirmed the property rights of the Pueblos. New towns began to spring up around these grants, including the towns of Santa Cruz in 1695 and Albuquerque in 1706.

During the course of the seventeenth century, the Spanish had placed a heavy emphasis on the Christianization of the Pueblos. Indeed, the missionary zeal of the Franciscan Order looms as one of the strongest motivations for the settlement of the province. But after the reconquest, Spanish royal policy placed a greater stress on the military defense of the northern outpost. In the face of threats by the French, who were expanding their trade network westward from Louisiana, and constant attacks by Plains Indians, Spain took action to strengthen its defenses. As part of a general administrative and military reorganization of the Indies, known as the Bourbon Reforms, a new jurisdictional unit was created, the *Provincias Internas,* comprising the present states of Texas, New Mexico, Arizona and California, as well as parts of northern Mexico.

Gradually, through the late eighteenth and early nineteenth centuries, the presence of English and United States explorers and traders began to replace the French as a source of concern to Spanish officials in New Mexico. By its defeat in the French and Indian War, France was expelled from the North American continent in 1763, leaving the English to face the Spanish across the Mississippi River. The successful war of independence fought by the fledgling United States led to a renewed Anglo-American interest in the Spanish southwest after 1783. Beginning in 1803, the year of the Louisiana Purchase, a series of expeditions sponsored by the new nation, including those of Lewis and Clark and Zebulon Pike, triggered alarms in the Spanish capital at Santa Fe. The road was now paved, it was feared, for these new intruders from the east to capture the rich silver mines of New Spain, as well as the lucrative markets of New Mexico.

With the independence of Mexico from Spain in 1821, those markets now became officially open for exploitation. The Spanish royal policy of protectionism was formally abandoned in favor of an open trading policy, and increasing numbers of traveling merchants set out from the east along the recently developed Santa Fe Trail, destined for New Mexico. The growing pains experienced by the new Mexican nation, most importantly the internal administrative chaos, rendered the northern provinces, including New Mexico, extremely vulnerable to external exploitation. The secession of Texas from the Republic of Mexico in 1836 and its subsequent annexation to the United States a few years later served to strain relationships between the U.S. and Mexico. Motivated by a feeling that it was the "Manifest Destiny" of the United States to possess the entire North American continent, a large segment of the U.S. population pushed for the annexation of the territory from New Mexico to California. In May of 1846, under a dubious pretext, President James K. Polk ordered the invasion of Mexico by U.S. troops, thus beginning the Mexican War. Three months later, General Stephen Watts

Kearny led a victorious U.S. Army unopposed across northern New Mexico and into Santa Fe. Kearny's conquest was formalized by the 1848 Treaty of Guadalupe Hidalgo, by which the U.S. paid Mexico 15 million dollars for New Mexico, Arizona and California. Under the terms of the Compromise of 1850, New Mexico was granted status as a Territory of the United States.

By the time the Guadalupe Hidalgo Treaty was ratified, gold had been discovered in California. Hundreds upon thousands left their homes and jobs and headed west to the gold fields. Many who began the journey, although interested in gold, sometimes were unable to continue their travel westward. They decided to settle in the territory of New Mexico.

Shortly after the Civil War began in the east, the Confederacy turned its attention to the southwest, particularly New Mexico and the mineral deposits in Colorado and California. The Santa Fe Trail was the most important supply route connecting the east with the west. The attack on New Mexico began when Confederate General Sibley marched up the Río Grande in February 1862 with 3300 troops from Texas and defeated the Union troops at Valverde. The Confederates then captured Albuquerque and Santa Fe and raised the Southern flag over the capital city. Two weeks later, the results were reversed in the Battle of Glorieta Pass in Apache Canyon when the Colorado Volunteers and troops from the New Mexico Volunteers defeated the Confederates, resulting in their retreat to El Paso.

The late nineteenth century witnessed a dramatic change in the pattern of land tenure in Territorial New Mexico. Although the Treaty of Guadalupe Hidalgo guaranteed the property rights of former Mexican citizens, problems in the interpretation of Spanish and Mexican land laws worked to the disadvantage of Hispanic landholders as well as Indian pueblos. Poorly defined boundaries and the lack of original documentation led the U.S. Office of the Surveyor General to dismiss many claims. New arrivals from the east and shrewd attorneys quickly took advantage of the situation by acquiring the valuable lands now made available to them. It was not until 1891 that a Court of Private Land Claims was established to review the actions of the Office of the Surveyor General. This step, too, proved less than adequate. As a result, suits concerning disputed land and water claims continue to appear in the courts in the 1980s.

By the Compromise of 1850, California became the thirty-first state. Later, Colorado, Kansas and Nebraska were admitted to the Union. New Mexico would be bypassed fifteen times before statehood was to be realized.

It was not until 1912 that the opposing forces were reconciled and New Mexico finally was admitted to the Union as the 47th state. At that time, it had a population of 330,000 living in a relatively peaceful and quiet area where farming and ranching flourished alongside a rapidly expanding mining industry. The discovery of oil introduced new manufacturing procedures and the automobile industry provided new outlets for petroleum. New methods in farming and ranching encouraged business prospects for the state. By 1937, tourism had become an important industry to New Mexico. It also opened the way for communication and exchange of ideas with other states and nations.

After World War II, the federal government provided funds to establish missile bases and experimental stations around the country. Los Alamos had been set up by the government during World War II as a secret facility to coordinate the Manhattan Project resulting in the development of the first atomic bomb. The choice was made to explode the bomb on a part of Alamogordo Bombing Range in the Jornada del Muerto. The code name was "Trinity Site." As a result of these early experiments, the first nuclear bomb was exploded on July 6, 1945 ushering in the Atomic Age. Later, Sandia National Laboratories (SNL), formerly Sandia Base, was established in Albuquerque to develop weapons for military use. Since that time, the facility has been involved with experimental programs such as the Nuclear Waste Isolation Pilot Project (WIPP). Los Alamos National Laboratories (LANL) is now experimenting in the peaceful application of nuclear energy and pioneering in thermonuclear sources of power. The Laboratory's Meson facility is engaged in cancer research.

Without doubt, New Mexico is a unique state. The diversity and complexity of its history, climate, topography and ethnic composition serve to make New Mexico a fascinating place to live and work. Many of the old ideas have given way to new ones. Nevertheless, large segments of the population still cling to their traditional ways of life. It is this interaction between progress and tradition that has shaped the development of New Mexico to the present day, and is likely to shape its future.

Donald R. Lavash, Ph.D.
Stanley M. Hordes, Ph.D.

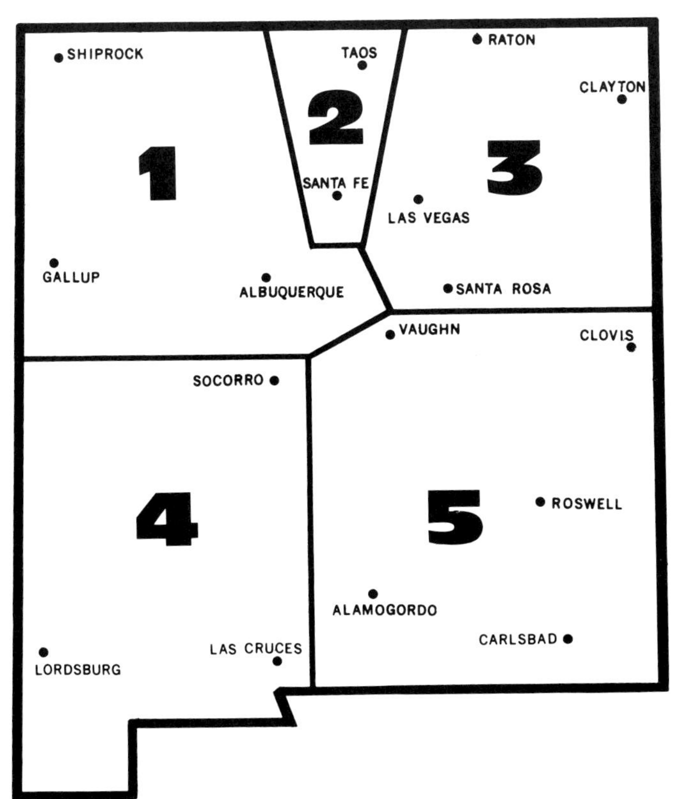

HOW BEST TO USE THIS BOOK

The text of the book covers all information given on the historical marker plates. The map of New Mexico has been divided into five districts or regions. Each of these regions has a number and can be located by referring to the key at the bottom of the map pages. Following each map, the text for the markers in that area is given. The numbers on the maps enclosed by a circle refer to the location of the Historical Markers and the text for these markers is arranged in the same numerical order. An alphabetical index covering the entire state and giving the map number and location is also included.

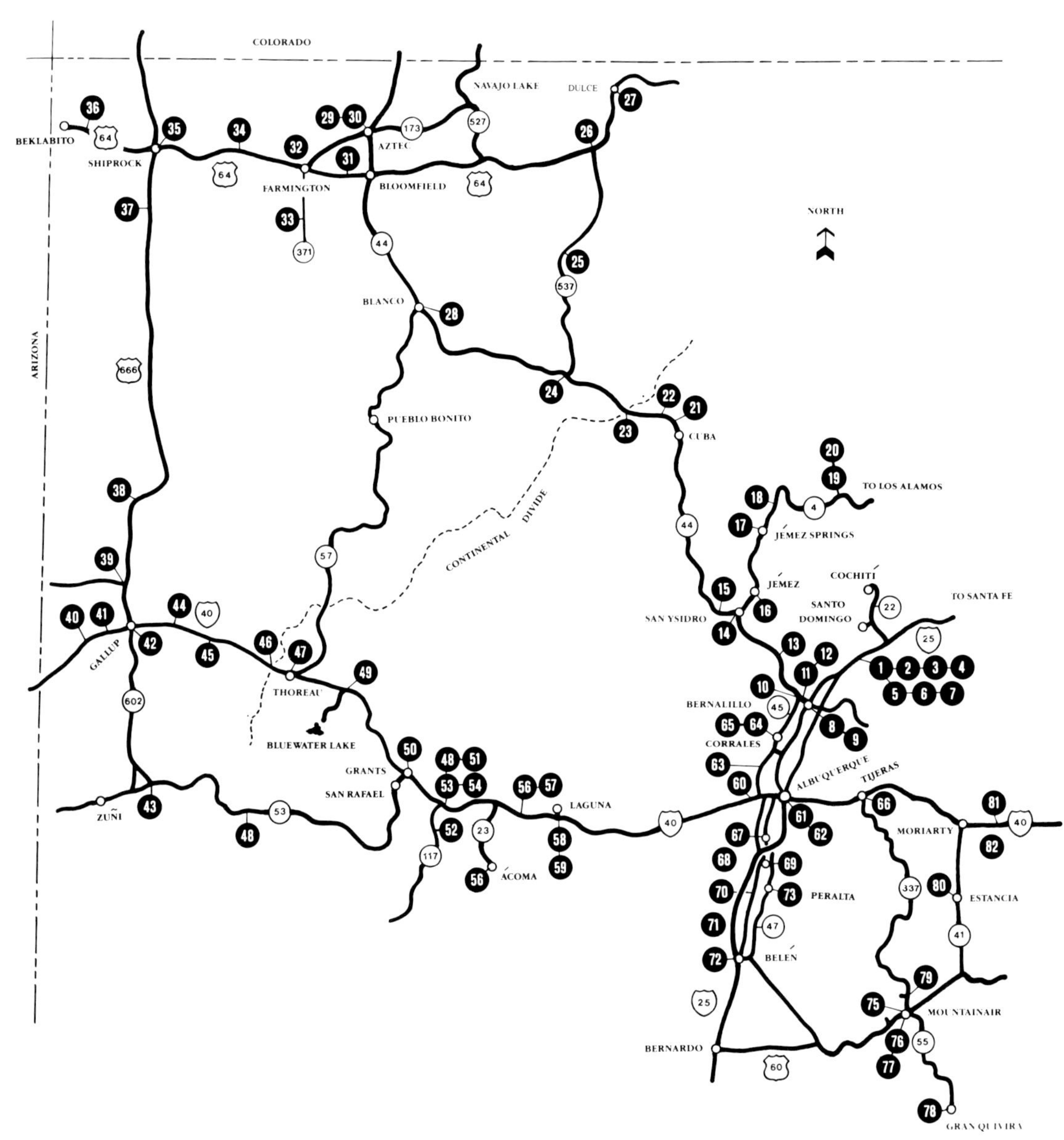

REGIONAL MAP NUMBER ONE

Map Symbols

Historical Markers . . . . 1—82

Interstate Highways . . . .

U.S. Highways . . . .

State Highways . . . .

Pueblo of Santo Domingo [1]

Gaspar Castaño de Sosa camped here in 1591, and in the 17th century Santo Domingo served as headquarters of the Franciscan Order in New Mexico. It has had several different churches. The present one was built around 1890 by Father Noël Dumarest, and retains the traditional ecclesiastical architecture of this region.

Pueblo of Cochití [2]

Cochití was established in the 1200s by Keresan-speaking Indians who came here from villages located at the present-day site of Bandelier National Monument. European contact was slight until Oñate's colonization in 1598. In the 1960s, the mission church of San Buenaventura de Cochití was restored to its nineteenth-century appearance.

Kearny's Route [3]

In 1846, U.S. forces under Brigadier General Stephen Watts Kearny invaded New Mexico and, on August 18, raised the U.S. flag in Santa Fe. Afterwards, he marched unopposed into Bernalillo and Albuquerque. As a result of this occupation, New Mexico passed from the jurisdiction of Mexico to that of the United States.

Pueblo of Santa Ana [4]

The Keres-speaking pueblo of Santa Ana was established on its present site in 1693, as part of Diego de Vargas' reconquest of New Mexico. The spot, exposed to flooding, was poorly suited for farming, and today the residents live on their farms along the Río Grande instead of the pueblo, which is used as a ceremonial site.

Pueblo Revolt Tricentennial [5]

On August 10, 1680 the Pueblo Indians rose in revolt against Spanish rule. Forced to evacuate Santa Fe by the Tanos, Tewas and Tiwas, Governor Otermín led the retreating colonists south through the lands of the Keres pueblos, whose signal fires could be seen on the mesas, passing through the Pueblo of Santo Domingo on August 24.

Pueblo of Sandía [6]

Sandía is one of the pueblos of the Tiguex Province visited by the Vásquez de Coronado expedition in 1540. Abandoned during the Pueblo Revolt of 1680, when many Tiwas fled to Hopi country, it was resettled by Tiwa-speaking refugees and a few Hopis in 1748. Its church, built in 1864, was renovated in 1976.

Pueblo of San Felipe [7]

San Felipe, named for St. Philip the Apostle by Spanish explorer Francisco Sánchez Chamuscado in 1581, was abandoned during the Pueblo Revolt of 1680. Reestablished on the mesa top, this too was abandoned before 1706, when the pueblo was constructed on its present site. The mission church appears today much as it did in the 18th century.

Bernalillo – On the Camino Real [8]

Population—2763   Elevation—5050 ft.

The Pueblo Indian province of Tiguex, in the area of Bernalillo, served as winter headquarters for Francisco Vásquez de Coronado in 1540-42 during his explorations of the southwest. Bernalillo was founded after the Spanish reconquest of New Mexico by Diego de Vargas in 1692. Vargas died here in 1704.

Tiguex Province [9]

More than one hundred prehistoric and historic pueblos and other archeological sites and over 15,000 petroglyphs or rock art sites give ample evidence of the occupation of this valley for at least 12,000 years. Spanish explorers who came into the area in the sixteenth century gave the name "Tiguex Province" to the dozen or more Tiwa-speaking Indian pueblos (towns) they found in the middle Rio Grande Valley.

Sandía Mountains [10]

A giant block of the earth's crust tipped up sideways, the Sandía Mountains are a range of the Basin and Range province in New Mexico. The adjoining Río Grande rift contains deep aquifers that provide water for the large population center of Albuquerque. Sandía Crest elevation is 10,678 feet.

Coronado State Monument [11]

Kuaua Pueblo was one of the Río Grande Valley villages visited by Francisco Vásquez de Coronado in 1540. He called this region the Tiguex Province because its inhabitants spoke a common language, Tiwa. Abandoned before the 1680 Pueblo Revolt against Spanish rule, this large and important site has been excavated and partially restored.

Spanish Entrada Site [12]

Among the many prehistoric and historic sites located nearby is a camp where Francisco Vasquez de Coronado's troops may have spent the winter of 1540-41. Coronado also visited the ancient pueblo of Kuaua located to the north. Kuaua's ruins are preserved and interpreted at the Coronado State Monument near Bernalillo.

Pueblo of Zía [13]

In 1583 Antonio de Espejo recorded this pueblo as one of five in the Province of Punamé. Following the sacking of Zía by Spanish troops in 1689, the pueblo was reestablished, but never attained its former size. The Zía ancient sun sumbol is incorporated in the design of the state flag of New Mexico.

Vásquez de Coronado's Route [14]

Francisco Vásquez de Coronado, preparing to spend his second winter in New Mexico, sent out expeditions from Tiguex, near Bernalillo, in the fall of 1541 to gather supplies. Captain Francisco de Barrionuevo went as far west as Jémez Pueblo, then visited others as far north as the Río Chama.

Colorado Plateau [15]

From this point, the Colorado Plateau extends across northwestern New Mexico into northeastern Arizona, southeastern Utah, and southwestern Colorado. A colorful landscape of mesas, and canyons, it is underlain by natural mineral, oil, and gas resources locked within sedimentary strata deposited millions of years ago. Elevation 6,400 feet.

Pueblo of Jémez [16]

Jémez is the sole surviving pueblo of the seven in the "provincia de los Hemes" noted by Spaniards in 1541, and the last at which the Towa language is still spoken. In 1838 the remaining inhabitants of Pecos Pueblo moved here. The mission of San Diego de Jémez was last rebuilt in the 1880s.

Jémez State Monument [17]

The village of Giusewa was occupied by ancestors of the Jémez Indians before the arrival of the Spanish in 1541. Its ruins lie close to those of the great stone mission church of San José de Giusewa, which was built by the Franciscans around 1622.

Soda Dam [18]

This spectacular formation has built up over the centuries by deposits of calcium carbonate from a spring that bubbles to the surface at this point. The river flows under a dome that is still building. The dam is 300 feet long, 50 feet high, and 50 feet wide at the bottom.

Valle Grande [19]

About one million years ago, the magnificent valley before you was formed by collapse, after a series of tremendous volcanic eruptions ejected a volume of material more than 500 times greater than the May 1980 eruptions of Mt. St. Helens. This event climaxed more than 13 million years of volcanism in the Jémez Mountains. Minor volumes of magma, leaking to the surface as recently as 50,000 years ago, formed the dome-like hills between you and the skyline to the north, which is the opposite wall of the enormous Valles Caldera. The heat from young volcanism makes this area attractive for geothermal energy.

Valle Grande [20]

Often called "the world's largest crater," Valle Grande is actually a giant caldera, formed a million years ago when a series of volcanoes collapsed, and whole mountains were engulfed forming the great valley below this highway.

San Juan Basin [21]

Thousands of feet of sedimentary strata have been downwarped into the San Juan basin of northwestern New Mexico, a total area of some 20,000 square miles. The San Pedro and Nacimiento Ranges of the Southern Rockies rise in fault contact above the basin to elevations of more than 10,000 feet.

Jicarilla Apache Reservation [22]

The Jicarilla Apaches, primarily a hunting and gathering group, once occupied vast portions of northeastern New Mexico and southern Colorado. Pressure from Comanche Indians and European settlers eventually pushed them from their homeland. In 1887, the Jicarillas were given a permanent reservation in north-central New Mexico, near Dulce.

Continental Divide [23]

Elevation 7379 feet

Rainfall divides at this point. To the west it drains into the Pacific Ocean, to the east, into the Atlantic.

Jicarilla Apache Reservation
Centennial Highway [24]

The Jicarilla Apache Reservation was established on February 11, 1887 by Executive Order of President Grover Cleveland. The Dulce area, then known as Amargo, had served as a reservation for the Jicarilla from 1882 to 1883, at which time they were removed to Mescalero, in southern New Mexico. The Jicarilla began their trek back from Mescalero on April 25, 1887 and arrived at their new homeland in early June 1887.

Jicarilla Apache Reservation
Centennial Highway [25]

The Jicarilla Apache, a Southern Athabascan people, migrated to the southwest from northwest Canada. The Jicarilla Apache's pre-reservation homeland ranged from southeastern Colorado through northeastern New Mexico, to the Texas/Oklahoma panhandle. The Jicarilla Apache, named by the Spanish for the reed baskets they wove, are composed of two clans - the Llanero (plains) and the Ollero (mountain).

Jicarilla Apache Reservation
Centennial Highway [26]

During the 19th century, the United States government attempted to establish reservations to separate Indian tribes from settlers along the frontier. The Jicarilla Apache initially agreed to settle on a reservation in 1851, but unratified treaties and local political squabbles hampered the process of obtaining a reservation for 36 years. President Grover Cleveland finally issued the Executive Order which established a permanent home for the Jicarilla on February 11, 1887.

Jicarilla Apache Reservation
Centennial Highway [27]

The Jicarilla Apache Tribe commemorated the Centennial Anniversary of their present reservation on February 11, 1987. The Centennial was also observed at the annual Little Beaver Pow-wow and Round-up in July and the Go-Jii-Ya Fiesta September 13-15. The Jicarilla Apache Centennial Wagon Trek, a 200 mile horse and wagon journey from Cimarron to Dulce, was undertaken May 26-June 14, 1987, to acknowledge earlier homelands around Cimarron, Taos, and Abiquiu.

Chaco Culture National Historical Park [28]

Chaco Canyon contains hundreds of sites documenting its Indian occupation from 5000 B.C. through the early 20th century. Most spectacular are a dozen large and excellently crafted masonry pueblos of the 11th and 12th centuries. After its abandonment around 1300, the canyon was settled by Navajos from the early 1700s until the 1940s.

Aztec [29]

Population—5512   Elevation—5460 ft.

Aztec, named for the nearby National Monument, was founded in 1876 when portions of the Jicarilla Apache Reservation were opened for non-Indian settlement. It is the seat of San Juan County, which was created in 1887 partially as a response to the desire of the residents to be free from the political forces of Río Arriba County.

Aztec Ruins National Monument [30]

Despite its name, this magnificent site reflects 11th century influence from nearby Chaco Canyon rather than from the later Aztecs of Mexico. The striking masonry pueblos illustrate the classic Chaco architectural style with later Mesa Verde additions. Aztec was finally abandoned by 1300.

Salmon Ruin [31]

In the late 11th century, influence from Chaco Canyon, 45 miles south of here, began to be felt at this site and at nearby Aztec Ruins National Monument. The Chacoans abandoned this large and well-built masonry pueblo by 1150, and shortly thereafter, Mesa Verde people reoccupied it for approximately fifty years.

Farmington [32]

Population—30,729   Elevation—5395 ft.

Until 1876 this area comprised part of the Jicarilla Apache Reservation. Anglo settlement quickly began at the confluence of the San Juan, Animas, and La Plata Rivers. Farmington became a ranching and farming area and, later, an important producer of oil, gas, coal, and uranium.

Bisti Wilderness [33]

The highly scenic badlands of the Bisti were created by the erosion and weathering of interbedded shale, sandstone and coal formations into unusual forms. The area is also rich in fossil flora and fauna. 3,946 acres of the Badlands were designated a Wilderness Area by Congress in 1984 to preserve their scenic and cultural value. The Wilderness is protected by federal law.

Hogback [34]

Steeply dipping strata define the western edge of the San Juan basin. To the west older geologic formations are exposed toward the Defiance uplift whereas basinward they are downwarped thousands of feet beneath younger rock units. Vast coal, uranium, oil and gas resources occur in the strata buried within the basin. Elevation 5,050 feet.

Shiprock [35]

This area has been part of the Navajo homeland for centuries. The town of Shiprock is named for the great peak nearby, which figures importantly in Navajo legend. Early in the 20th century, Shiprock was made headquarters of the Northern Navajo Agency.

Beclabito Dome [36]

Colorful red rocks of Entrada Sandstone are domed up by deep seated igneous intrusions to be exposed by erosion. The same igneous activity created the Carrizo Mountains to the west. Uranium deposits in the Morrison Formation just above the Entrada created New Mexico's first uranium boom in the East Carrizos south of here in the 1950's. Elevation 5,600 feet.

Shiprock [37]

This huge volcanic neck was formed in Pliocene time, over 3,000,000 years ago. It rises 1700 feet above the surrounding plain and is famed in the legends of the Navajo as ''Sa-bit-tai-e'' (the rock with the wings). They hold that it was the great bird that brought them from the north.

Navajo Indian Reservation [38]

Occupants of northwest New Mexico since the 16th century, the Navajos today comprise the most populous Indian group in the United States. The 17th, 18th and 19th centuries witnessed alternate periods of conflict and trading with their neighbors. The Navajos' economy traditionally has been based on stockraising, weaving, silversmithing, and more recently on mineral development.

Fort Defiance [39]

Now in the State of Arizona but then in the Territory of New Mexico, Fort Defiance was once described as ''the most beautiful and interesting post as a whole in New Mexico.'' It was established in 1851 to control the Navajos, and abandoned as a military post in 1864.

Manuelito Area [40]

This area contained many Indian pueblos dating from about A.D. 500 to 1325, when it was abandoned. Navajos settled here by 1800. This was the home of Manuelito, one of the last of the chiefs to surrender for confinement at the Bosque Redondo Reservation near Fort Sumner. The Navajos returned here in 1868.

Vásquez de Coronado's Route [41]

In July 1540, Francisco Vásquez de Coronado, leader of an army of Spaniards and Indians, entered New Mexico from Arizona to the south of here. He was searching for the mythical Seven Cities of Cíbola, which proved to be the six Zuñi villages then located near the present pueblo. Vásquez de Coronado was nearly killed during his attack on Hawikuh.

Gallup [42]

Population—18,161   Elevation—6600 ft.

Long a major trading center for the Navajo and Zuñi Indians living in communities north and south of the town, Gallup emerged in 1881 from a railroad construction camp. It is named for David Gallup, who in 1880 was paymaster for the Atlantic & Pacific (now the Santa Fe) Railroad.

Pueblo of Zuñi [43]

The six original Zuñi pueblos were the legendary "Seven Cities of Cíbola" sought by Vásquez de Coronado in 1540. They were abandoned during the Pueblo Revolt, and the present pueblo was settled in 1699 after the Spanish reconquest. In 1970, Zuñi became the first Indian community to administer its own reservation affairs.

Fort Wingate [44]

The first Fort Wingate was established near San Rafael in 1862, to serve as the base of Col. Kit Carson's campaigns against the Navajos. In 1868 the garrison was transferred to the second Fort Wingate near Gallup. In that same year, the Navajos returned here after their imprisonment at Fort Sumner.

Chaco Cliffs [45]

Great cliffs of red sandstone form the southern boundary of the San Juan basin. The strata exposed here are the gently upturned edge of the structural basin which contains coal, uranium, oil and gas resources. The Zuñi Mountains to the south represent the old basement rock upon which the basin strata were deposited. Elevation is 6,900 feet.

Continental Divide [46]

Elevation 7245 feet

Rainfall divides at this point. To the west it drains into the Pacific Ocean, to the east, into the Atlantic.

Chaco Culture National Historical Park [47]

Chaco Canyon contains hundreds of sites documenting its Indian occupation from 5000 B.C. through the early 20th century. Most spectacular are a dozen large and excellently crafted masonry pueblos of the 11th and 12th centuries. After its abandonment around 1300, the canyon was settled by Navajos from the early 1700s until the 1940s.

El Morro National Monument Inscription Rock [48]

Until it was by-passed by the railroad in the 1880s, its waterhole made El Morro an important stop for travelers in the Ácoma-Zuñi region. Numerous inscriptions carved in the sandstone date from the prehistoric, Spanish, Mexican, and Territorial periods in New Mexico's history. An important example is Oñate's inscription, carved in 1605.

Mount Taylor [49]

One of the great volcanic cones of the Colorado Plateau, Mount Taylor rises to an elevation of 11,301 feet and last erupted some 2 million years ago. Numerous fissure eruptions since that time and as recently as about 1,200 years ago have created lava flows that form malpais or badlands along portions of this route. Elevation here 6,550 feet.

Grants [50]

Population—11,451   Elevation—6500 ft.

Located just north of the great lava bed known as the malpais, Grants began as a coaling station for the Santa Fe Railroad. Around 1880 it was known as Grant's Camp, after the Canadian bridge contractor Angus A. Grant. In 1950, the area's vast uranium deposits were discovered.

San Rafael [51]

San Rafael, formerly known as El Gallo, is located at a spring near the Malpais, the great lava flow to the east. The area was visited by members of Vásquez de Coronado's expedition in 1540. In 1862, it was selected as the original site of Fort Wingate, focus of the campaign against the Navajos.

Kowina [52]

Kowina is one of the ancestral Acoma pueblos, occupied from approximately 1100-1200 A.D. This and several ancient pueblos on the Cebolleta Mesa and surrounding area were established when smaller settlements began to congregate and withdraw into larger, more easily defensible sites as early as 950 A.D. The Kowina Cultural Research Foundation was located here in the early 1970's.

Lava Beds [53]

This is the narrowest stretch of lava flow that extends almost 25 miles to the southwest where it originated about 1,000 years ago from a volcanic vent. Here the flow fills an old river valley where numerous dry and water-filled pockets are associated with pressure ridges and areas of collapsed lava tubes.

Pueblo Revolt Tricentennial [54]

The western pueblos of Ácoma and Zuñi took part in the revolt against Spanish rule which broke out on August 10, 1680. During the 1690s refugees from the Río Grande pueblos, escaping from reconquest of their lands, joined with local Keresans to form the Pueblo of Laguna.

Old Acoma "Sky City" [55]

Legend describes Acoma as a "place that always was". Archeological evidence shows it has been occupied since at least the 13th century. Established on this mesa for defensive purposes, Acoma was settled by inhabitants of nearby pueblos which had been abandoned. Nearly destroyed by the Spanish in 1599, Acoma was quickly reestablished by ancestors of its present occupants.

Pueblo of Ácoma [56]

Built atop a great mesa for defensive purposes, Ácoma has been continuously occupied since the 13th century. A dramatic battle between the Ácomas and Oñate's forces occurred here in 1599. The mission church of San Esteban was built between 1629 and 1641, and today looks much as described by Fray Francisco Atanasio Domínguez in 1776.

Cebolleta [57]

In 1749 a Navajo mission was established at Cebolleta, and by 1804, Albuquerque area stockmen had built a fortified town for themselves. During the resulting warfare, the Spanish settlers used Los Portales Cave as a refuge. The cave was later converted to a shrine with an altar carved from the living rock.

San José de la Laguna Mission [58]

The picturesque mission church of San José de la Laguna was built around 1706 by Fray Antonio Miranda and shows the single-aisle floor plan commonly used in pueblo churches. It has been repaired many times, and acquired its distinctive white stucco exterior in 1977.

The church contains a beautiful and well-preserved altar screen made between 1800 and 1808 by a folk artist known only as the "Laguna santero." The interior walls are mud-plastered and white-washed, and the floor is made of packed earth. The handsome wooden ceiling is laid in a herringbone pattern.

Pueblo of Laguna [59]

Keresan-speaking refugees from Santo Domingo, Ácoma, Cochití, and other pueblos founded Laguna after the Pueblo Revolt of 1680 and the Spanish reconquest of 1692. Named by the Spaniards for a marshy lake to the west, the pueblo still occupies its original hilltop site today.

Río Grande Rift [60]

Albuquerque is situated at the juncture of two major blocks in the earth's crust. One block, the Sandía Mountains, is tilted upward toward the east along the Sandía fault. West of the fault, the Río Grande rift has dropped downward forming a great trough which has subsided 26,000 feet from the rim of the mountains.

Albuquerque – On the Camino Real [61]

Population—331,767   Elevation—5310 ft.

Spanish settlers had lived here before the Pueblo Revolt of 1680, but the area was resettled when the "Villa de Alburquerque" was founded in 1706. In addition to promoting colonization, the new town was intended to provide protection from attacks by Indians in Río Abajo, or lower Río Grande Valley.

Old Town Plaza – On the Camino Real [62]

The center of Albuquerque's Old Town, the plaza dates from the early 18th century. San Felipe de Neri Church was established in 1706, but construction of the present structure was begun in 1793. In March 1862, General Henry H. Sibley and his Texas volunteers occupied Albuquerque and raised the Confederate flag here.

Albuquerque Petroglyphs [63]

Over 15,000 petroglyphs have been carved into the lava rock which covers the mesa west of the Rio Grande. The earliest of these rock drawings were made by prehistoric inhabitants almost 3000 years ago. Many others were added by Pueblo peoples and later by Spanish explorers and settlers. This gallery of ancient art is interpreted at Petroglyph State Park 6 miles south of here.

Corrales [64]

Population—2791   Elevation—5,097 ft.

Spanish colonization of this region, once the location of many Tiwa Indian pueblos, began in the 17th century. Corrales is named for the extensive corrals built here by Juan González, founder of Alameda. In the 18th century this rich farming area was subject to Comanche attacks, and was raided by Navajos as late as 1851.

San Isidro, patron saint of farmers, is the traditional guardian of the valley. The present church is the third to bear his name. Spanish, and later, United States garrisons used the valley as a base of defense to protect the river settlements of Albuquerque and Bernalillo, and nearby pueblos and towns from Navajo raids.

Iglesia De San Ysidro [65]

This church was constructed in 1868 following a flood which demolished an earlier building. Dedicated to San Ysidro, patron of farmers, the church incorporates materials salvaged from the original structure. The building is one of the finest surviving examples of mid-19th century New Mexico religious architecture. It is maintained by the Corrales Historical Society and used for community functions and other cultural events.

Tijeras Canyon [66]

This pass between the Sandía and Manzano Mountains has been a natural route for travel between eastern New Mexico and the Río Grande Valley since prehistoric times. Known as Cañon de Carnué in the Spanish colonial period, it takes its present name from the village of Tijeras, Spanish for "scissors".

Los Padillas [67]

Los Padillas is an extended family settlement which was resettled in 1718 by Diego de Padilla. His grandparents had lived on the site prior to the 1680 Pueblo Revolt at which time they were forced to abandon it. In the 1790 census the town, referred to as San Andres de los Padillas, had a population of 168. This is the site of the old Los Padillas School, originally built in 1901 and replaced in 1912.

Old Armijo School [68]

Constructed in 1914, this building was designed by Atanacio Montoya, a progressive educator who introduced many reforms into early 20th century rural schools. It served as the school for the Village of Armijo until 1948. This school incorporated architectural features that were considered quite innovative and advanced for its time and is the only surviving structure of its kind.

Pueblo of Isleta [69]

Isleta, or "little island" in Spanish, is the largest of the Río Grande pueblos. Many Isletans moved to El Paso with the Spanish during the 1680 Revolt; others resettled the pueblo around 1710. Parts of the mission, San Agustín de la Isleta, date from about 1613.

Vásquez de Coronado's Route [70]

In the fall of 1540, Francisco Vásquez de Coronado's army traveled from Zuñi to his chosen winter headquarters in the Tiguex province on the Río Grande. Here the advance guard of the army followed the river from the Isleta area to Alcanfor, a pueblo near Bernalillo, where it camped for two winters.

Dennis Chavez Highway [71]

United States highway 85, which parallels Interstate 25 the length of New Mexico from Texas to Colorado, was designated "Dennis Chavez Highway" in 1988 to honor the long and meritorious service of New Mexico's first native-born United States Senator, Dennis Chavez (1888-1962). First elected to Congress in 1930, Chavez was serving his fifth consecutive term as United States Senator at the time of his death in 1962.

Belén – On the Camino Real [72]

Population—5617   Elevation—4800 ft.

By the mid 18th century, Spanish colonization had begun along the Río Grande south of Albuquerque. The Belén land grant was made to encourage this expansion, and colonists from Albuquerque settled here around 1740. The early community also included a group of genízaros, or Hispanicized Indians. Belén is Spanish for Bethlehem.

Peralta [73]

One of the last skirmishes of the Civil War in New Mexico took place here on April 15, 1862. The Sibley Brigade, retreating to Texas, camped at the hacienda of Governor Henry Connelly, a few miles from Peralta. Here the Confederates were routed by Union forces under Col. Edward R.S. Canby.

Tajique [74]

The pueblo-mission of San Miguel de Tajique was established in the 1620's. In the 1670's, famine, disease and Apache raids caused the abandonment of the Jurisdiccion de las Salinas (1598-1678) which included Tajique. Modern occupation of Tajique began in the 1830's with a land grant made to Manuel Sanchez.

Abó Ruins [75]
Salinas National Monument

Located adjacent to the major east-west trade route through Abó Pass, the Tompiro Pueblo of Abó (ca. 1300s-1670s) was one of the Southwest's largest Pueblo Indian villages. Extensive Indian house complexes are dominated by the unique buttressed walls, 40 feet high, of the Spanish Franciscan mission church of San Gregorio de Abó, built around 1630.

Mountainair [76]

Population—1170   Elevation—6535 ft.

Founded in 1902, Mountainair developed as a major center for pinto bean farming in the early 20th century until the drought of the 1940s. The region had been occupied earlier by Tompiro and eastern Tiwa pueblo Indians from prehistoric times through the mid-17th century, when it served as a major center for Spanish Franciscan missionaries.

Salinas National Monument [77]

This unique regional complex of prehistoric Indian pueblos and associated 17th-century Franciscan mission ruins constitutes a "capsule in time" in which the first century of Native American-European contact in what is now the U.S. is preserved. Nearby are the Abó, Quarai, and Gran Quivira ruins. The central visitor center is in Mountainair's historic Shaffer Hotel.

Gran Quivira Ruins [78]
Salinas National Monument

The Tompiro Indian "Pueblo de las Humanas" (ca. 1300—1670s) had 1,500 to 2,000 inhabitants and was a trading center with Plains Indians. The village evolved for centuries on the fringe of the Mogollon and Anasazi cultures. There are two large Spanish Franciscan mission churches, San Isidro built in 1629, and San Buenaventura constructed in 1659.

Quarai Ruins [79]
Salinas National Monument

On the edge of the Plains stands the abandoned Tiwa Pueblo Indian village of Quarai (ca. 1200—1670s), the southernmost of the Tiwa villages, located along the eastern flanks of the Manzano Mountains. The Spanish Franciscan mission church of La Purísima Concepción (1630) is the most complete remaining example of the large Salinas churches.

Estancia [80]

Population—830   Elevation—6107 ft.

Incorporated in 1909 and county seat of Torrance County since 1905, Estancia is located in an enclosed valley or basin. It was ranching country until the early 20th century, when the coming of the railroad opened it to homesteaders and farmers. Pinto beans were the best known local crop until the 1950s.

Josiah Gregg, merchant and pioneer historian of the Santa Fe Trail, made four expeditions to Santa Fe. On his last, in 1839—40, he blazed a new route from Van Buren, Arkansas, which followed the Canadian River north of here. The new trail became popular with California-bound gold-seekers in 1849.

This large valley was occupied by ancient Ice Age Lake Estancia some 12,000 years ago. To the north, the Southern Rockies rise to altitudes of 13,000 feet; to the northwest are the Ortiz and San Pedro Mountains; to the west are the Sandia Mountains, and to the southwest are the Manzano Mountains. Elevation 6,200 feet.

Quarai Ruins
Salinas National Monument, No. 79, page 12

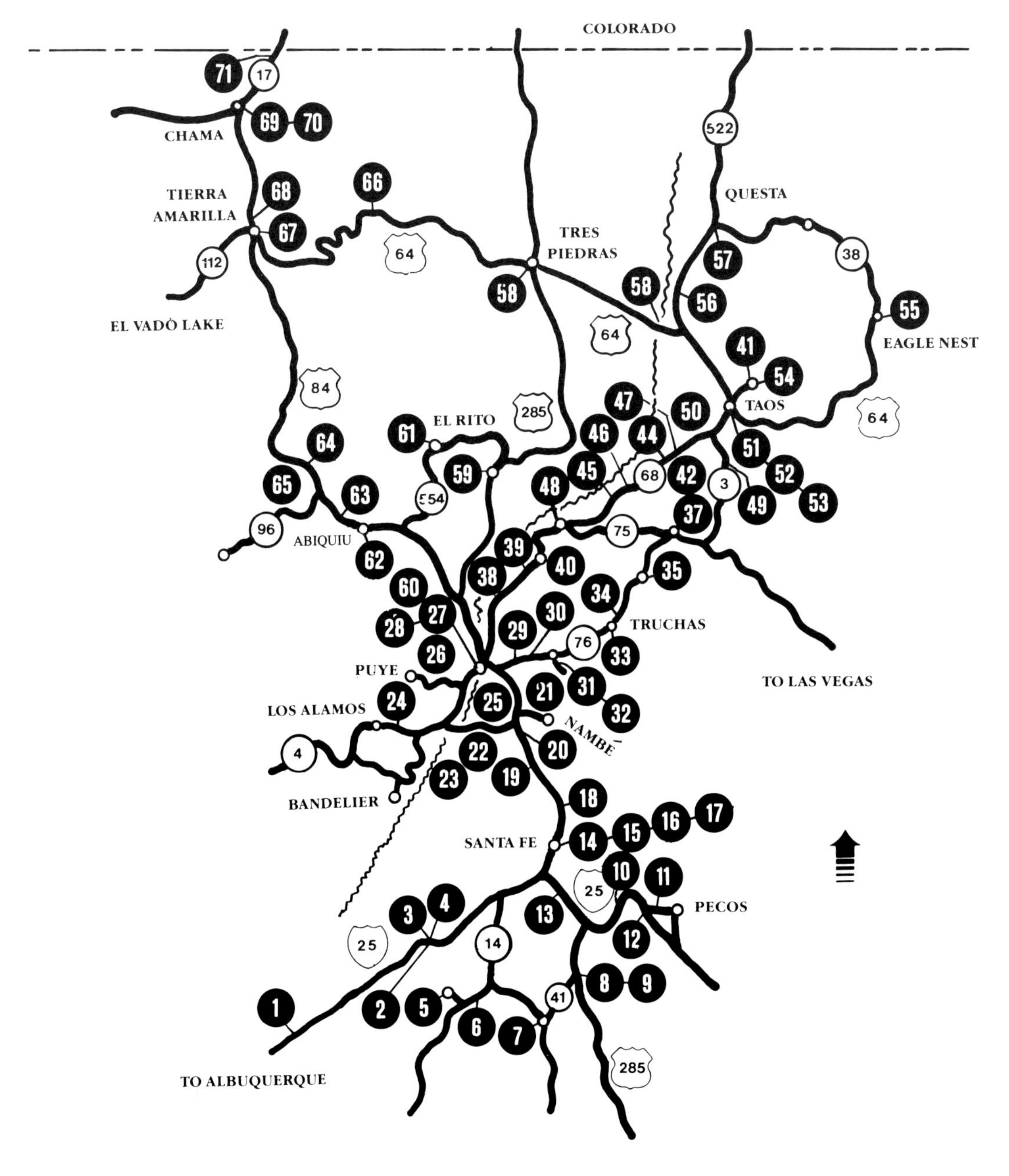

REGIONAL MAP NUMBER TWO

Map Symbols

Historical Markers . . . . **1**—**71**

Interstate Highways . . . .

U.S. Highways . . . .

State Highways . . . .

SANTA FE PLAZA . CIRCA 1880

La Bajada [1]

La Bajada, or "the descent," marks the division between the Río Arriba, or "upper river," and the Río Abajo, or "lower river," sections of New Mexico. This steep and dangerous grade was long an obstacle to caravan traffic going from the Río Grande Valley to Santa Fe.

La Bajada ("the descent") [2]

La Bajada Hill is a major break in topography situated along a geological fault zone that separates the downfaulted Río Grande rift from the Santa Fe Plateau. The red formation tilted at various angles along the fault zone is the Galisteo Formation deposited in streams about 70 million years ago.

More recent volcanic lavas form the resistant caprock of the plateau above. Landslide deposits are prominent on the slopes below the lava cap. Total relief from the rim of the Santa Fe Plateau to Galisteo Creek at the foot of La Bajada is about 800 feet.

Gold and Turquoise [3]

First gold placer mining west of the Mississippi began with the discovery of the precious metal in the rugged Ortiz Mountains south of here in 1828, 21 years before the California gold rush. Since then, the district has produced more than 99,000 ounces of placer gold. Gold is currently produced from lode deposits.

The prominent hills to the east and to the left are the Cerrillos Hills, site of ancient turquoise mines worked by the Indians centuries before the arrival of the Spanish. The Cerrillos ("little hills") are regarded as the oldest mining district in the United States, and New Mexico is a major turquoise producer. Elevation 6,200 feet.

South End of the Rockies [4]

Divided by the Río Grande, the volcanic Jémez Mountains are the western New Mexico Rockies; the Sangre de Cristo ("blood of Christ") Mountains are the eastern chain. Ice Age glaciers carved their summits including Santa Fe Baldy, the prominent peak in the Santa Fe Range which rises to 12,622 feet above sea level.

Cerrillos [5]

Elevation—5688

Before the arrival of the Spanish, the mineral-rich area around Cerrillos produced turquoise which was traded as far as the Valley of Mexico. An early settlement of Los Cerrillos harbored Spanish refugees from the 1680 Revolt, but the present community was not founded until the lead strike of 1879.

Garden of the Gods [6]

Vertical beds of colorful sandstone and mudstone of the Galisteo Formation were deposited in streams 70 million years ago. Deposited as horizontal sheets, they have been tilted to their present vertical position by mountain building forces beneath the earth's surface. Elevation 6,000 feet.

Galisteo Pueblo [7]

Spanish explorers found several Tano-speaking pueblos in the Galisteo Basin in 1540. They were among the leaders of the Pueblo Revolt of 1680. 150 Tano families were eventually resettled in Galisteo Pueblo in 1706. Droughts, famine, Comanche raids, and disease led to its abandonment by 1788, with most of the survivors moving to Santo Domingo.

Galisteo Basin [8]

The extensive lowland south of here is called the Galisteo basin, a sag in the earth's crust where rock layers are depressed and thickened. It is one of the northernmost basins of the Basin and Range province in New Mexico and is bordered by the Rocky Mountains immediately to the north. Elevation 6,400 feet.

Southern Rockies [9]

These foothills and the higher glaciated peaks to the north are the southern tip of the Rocky Mountains. This particular segment is known as the Sangre de Cristo ("blood of Christ"), a formidable barrier that rises above 13,000 feet in a chain of peaks that trend from Santa Fe on the south to Salida, Colorado on the north.

Cañoncito at Apache Canyon [10]

Strategically located where the Santa Fe Trail emerges from Glorieta Pass, this is where Mexican Governor Manuel Armijo prepared to defend New Mexico against the American Army in 1846. Here too, Union forces destroyed a Confederate supply train on March 28, 1862 while the Battle of Glorieta was in progress six miles to the east.

Glorieta Battlefield [11]

The decisive battle of the Civil War in New Mexico was fought at the summit of Glorieta Pass on March 28, 1862. Union troops won the battle when a party of Colorado volunteers burned the Confederate supply wagons, thus destroying Southern hopes for taking over New Mexico.

Glorieta Pass [12]

This pass served as a gateway through the mountains for Francisco Vásquez de Coronado in 1541 enroute to explore the plains, for Spanish friars attempting to convert Plains Indian tribes in the 1600s, for Apaches and Comanches entering the Pueblo area from the east, and for the Santa Fe Trail from the 1820s to 1880s.

Seton Village [13]

Ernest Thompson Seton (1860-1946), naturalist, artist, writer, authority on Indian lore, and first Chief Scout of the Boy Scouts of America, lived here during the last part of his life. The village includes his home, art collection, library, and Indian museum.

Santa Fe - On the Camino Real [14]

Population—48,899   Elevation—7045 ft.

Santa Fe, the oldest capital city in the United States, was established in 1610 as the seat of Spanish colonial government for the Province of New Mexico. The Palace of the Governors, used by Spanish, Mexican, and Territorial governors, has flanked the historic plaza since its construction in 1610, and now comprises part of the Museum of New Mexico.

San Isidro Catholic Church [15]

This 19th century adobe church is dedicated to San Isidro the ploughman, patron saint of farmers and protector of crops. Christian tradition maintains that in order to allow San Isidro time for his daily prayers, an angel plowed his fields. Agua Fria observes the fifteenth of May as "His Day of Goodwill" to honor his role in this agricultural community along El Camino Real..

Iglesia De San Isidro [15]

Esta iglesia fue construida en el siglo XIX y dedicada a San Isidro, patron de los labradores y protector de la cosecha. Tradicion Cristiana dice que un angel barbecho la tierra mientras San Isidro rezaba. La communidad de Agua Fria cada año celebra el quince de Mayo como "Dia de Benevolencia", en respeto de su ayuda a este pueblo labrador a lo largo del Camino Real.

Santuario De Guadalupe [16]

This adobe church, built sometime between 1776 and 1795, is the oldest shrine to Our Lady of Guadalupe in the United States. Its canvas painting of Our Lady is an outstanding example of Spanish ecclesiastical art. No longer an active church, the building is now a unique museum depicting New Mexico's religious history and is used for concerts and other community activities.

Museum of Fine Arts [17]

The Museum of Fine Arts opened in 1917. It was patterned after several early Franciscan missions in New Mexico. The Museum displays exhibits and serves as a center for performing arts events. The Museum of International Folk Art, Laboratory of Anthropology and Palace of the Governors are other units of the Museum of New Mexico in Santa Fe.

Pueblo of Tesuque [18]

The small Tewa-speaking pueblo of Tesuque was established around 1300, and was first visited by Europeans in 1591. The Pueblo Revolt, which drove the Spanish from New Mexico for thirteen years, broke out here in 1680. Its present church was built in the 1880s, on the foundations of an earlier structure.

Pueblo Revolt Tricentennial [19]

The Tewa pueblos of San Juan, San Ildefonso, Santa Clara, Pojoaque, Nambé and Tesuque were responsible for directing the 1680 Pueblo Revolt after the Spaniards captured two Indian runners at Tesuque on August 9. Joined by Taos and Picurís they formed into two divisions and on August 15 laid seige to Santa Fe.

Bandelier National Monument [20]

Thought to be an early home of Indians from Cochití and other Keres-speaking pueblos, the villages and cliff houses of Frijoles Canyon were occupied from the 1200s to before the arrival of the Spaniards in 1540. The monument is named for Adolph F. Bandelier, explorer and pioneer anthropologist of the Pajarito Plateau.

Pueblo of Nambé [21]

Occupied since about 1300, this Tewa pueblo was first described by Castaño de Sosa in 1591 as a square structure, two stories high, with a central plaza, whose people irrigated their crops. By the 18th century its population had dropped to 6 or 7 families. The present church of San Francisco de Nambé was built in 1974.

Jémez Mountains [22]

On the skyline to the west are the Jémez Mountains where tremendous volcanic eruptions a million years ago created a huge caldera some 15 miles in diameter that now forms beautiful Valle Grande set amid a ring of volcanic peaks. Geothermal energy has been tapped from hot rock beneath the mountains.

Flow and ash-fall deposits surrounding the volcanic range form the Pajarito Plateau, site of numerous, ancient cliff dwellings and the atomic city of Los Alamos. The Jémez Mountains are part of the Southern Rockies and form one of the western ranges of the Rockies in New Mexico. Elevations exceed 11,000 feet.

Pueblo of San Ildefonso [23]

In the 1500s, migrants from the Pajarito Plateau joined their Tewa-speaking relatives at San Ildefonso. The pueblo is famous as the home of the late María Martínez and other makers of polished black pottery. The modern church, a replica of that of 1711, was finished in 1968.

Los Alamos [24]

Population—17,599   Elevation—7324 ft.

Located near the ancient Indian sites of the Pajarito Plateau, Los Alamos is one of New Mexico's newest towns. In 1942 a boys' ranch school became the headquarters of the Manhattan Project, which led to the development of the atomic bomb. Los Alamos National Laboratories continues to be a center for nuclear and other scientific research.

Puyé Ruins [25]

This spectacular site on the Pajarito Plateau is located in the reservation of Santa Clara Pueblo. It includes a pueblo on the mesa top and rooms cut from the volcanic rock. Puyé, occupied from about 1250 to 1550, is considered the ancestral home of Santa Clara and other Tewa-speaking pueblos.

Pueblo of Santa Clara [26]

Founded around the fourteenth century, Santa Clara traces its ancestry to Puyé, an abandoned site of cave dwellings on the Pajarito Plateau. Increasing tensions with the Spanish led to its participation in the Pueblo Revolt of 1680. The mission church, once thought to be the narrowest of its kind, has been reconstructed several times since the 17th century.

Española Valley [27]

When it was described by Gaspar Castaño de Sosa in 1591, the Española Valley contained about ten Tewa-speaking pueblos, several of which are still occupied today. Juan de Oñate established New Mexico's first colony here in 1598. Long on the northern frontier of Spanish settlement, the Valley has continuously reflected its Indian and Spanish heritage.

The Bond House [28]

Frank Bond (1863-1945), prominent Española merchant, came from Canada in 1882. In 1887 Bond married May Anna Caffal of Pueblo, Colorado and built the home. The house grew from a two-room adobe to this large structure. Acquired by the city in 1957, the building is used as a museum today.

Santa Cruz de la Cañada [29]

In 1695, Governor Diego de Vargas founded his first town, Santa Cruz de la Cañada, designed to protect the Spanish frontier north of Santa Fe. The church, which still stands, was constructed in the 1730s. In 1837, residents revolted against Mexican authorities, resulting in the death of Governor Albino Pérez.

Santa Cruz Plaza –On the Camino Real [30]

In 1695 Governor Diego de Vargas founded Santa Cruz de la Cañada south of the Santa Cruz river. The town was later moved to this site north of the river. The church facing the plaza dates from the 1730s. Santa Cruz was an important stop on the Camino Real between Santa Fe and Taos.

Chimayó [31]

Indians occupied the Chimayó valley centuries before the arrival of the Spaniards. The village of Chimayó, founded in the early 18th century, shortly after the reconquest of New Mexico, has been a center of the Spanish weaving tradition for over 250 years. The village retains the historical pattern of settlement around a defensible plaza.

Santuario de Chimayó [32]

In 1816, Bernardo Abeyta and the other residents of El Potrero, then a separate community, finished this massive adobe chapel honoring Nuestro Señor de Esquípulas. It is noted for its 6-foot crucifix and its tradition of healing the sick. The Santuario remained in the Abeyta family until the 1920s.

SANTUARIO DE CHIMAYÓ

Truchas [33]

In 1754, Governor Tomás Vélez Cachupín granted land on the Río Truchas to families from Santa Cruz and Chimayó. Because Nuestra Señora del Rosario de Truchas was on the northern frontier, and subject to attack by Plains Indians, the governor stipulated that the houses should form a square with only one entrance.

Truchas Peaks [34]

Ice age glaciers carved these beautiful alpine peaks, among the highest in the New Mexico Rockies, rising to 13,101 feet. Precambrian quartzite, some of the oldest rock in New Mexico, forms the core of the Truchas ("trout") Peaks, part of the Pecos Wilderness which encompasses some of the most pristine mountain terrain in the state.

Las Trampas [35]

The village of Las Trampas was established in 1751 by 12 families from Santa Fe, led by Juan de Argüello, who received a land grant from Governor Tomás Vélez Cachupín. The Church of San José de Gracia is one of the finest surviving 18th-century churches in New Mexico.

Las Trampas [36]

La población de Las Trampas fue establecida en el año de 1751 con doce familias de la Villa de Santa Fe, conducidas por Juan de Argüello. Los pobladores recivieron una merced para este lugar del Gobernador Tomás Vélez Cachupín. La iglesia de San José de Gracia, que fue construida en el siglo diez y ocho, es una de las mas finas que se hallan en Nuevo México.

Pueblo of Picurís [37]

The pueblo of Picurís, first visited by Spaniards in 1591, was described as being 7 to 8 stories high. In the 18th century Picurís cooperated with the Spaniards against the raids of the Plains Indians. The church, the third at this pueblo, dates from the 1770s.

Pueblo of San Juan [38]

The first church in New Mexico was dedicated here in 1598 when Juan de Oñate used the pueblo as his headquarters. Popé, leader of the Pueblo Revolt of 1680, was from San Juan. The unusual Gothic-style church was built in 1912-13 by Father Camilo Seux, a French priest.

San Gabriel --On the Camino Real [39]

Governor Juan de Oñate set up his headquarters in San Juan Pueblo in 1598, but by 1601 he had moved the Spanish capital across the Río Grande to Yuque-Yunque Pueblo. Named San Gabriel, it served as the seat of government until 1610, when Oñate's successor founded a new capital at Santa Fe.

Velarde - On the Camino Real [40]

Founded in 1875, this small farming community was first named La Jolla. It was once famous for finely woven blankets. Here the Camino Real left the Río Grande and followed a canyon northeast to Embudo Creek where it began a climb over the mountains to Taos.

Taos Canyon [41]

In 1692, after having been driven from New Mexico by the Pueblo Revolt of 1680, the Spanish began to re-establish their rule. In one of the last battles of the reconquest, in September 1696, Governor Diego de Vargas defeated the Indians of Taos Pueblo at nearby Taos Canyon.

Sangre de Cristo ("Blood of Christ") [42]

From left to right along the eastern horizon, two of New Mexico's highest mountain ranges are visible . the Truchas Range and the Santa Fe Range. Both are part of the Sangre de Cristo Mountains of the Southern Rockies where glacier carved alpine peaks rise to elevations exceeding 13,000 feet.

Jémez Mountains [43]

Formed from cataclysmic volcanic eruptions some one million years ago, the Jémez Mountains are part of the westernmost New Mexico Rockies that enter the state from Colorado near Chama. Chicoma Peak (11,561 feet), prominent on the western horizon, is the highest in the Jémez Mountains. Elevation here 5,800 feet.

Pilar [44]

In 1795, twenty-five families were granted land along the Río Grande at Pilar, then known as Cieneguilla. The Battle of Cieneguilla was fought at Embudo Mountain near here in March 1854. A large force of Utes and Jicarilla Apaches inflicted heavy losses on sixty dragoons from Cantonment Burgwin near Taos.

Vásquez de Coronado's Route [45]

Under orders from Francisco Vásquez de Coronado in 1540, Captain Hernando de Alvarado explored among the pueblos and followed this route from Española to the Pueblo of Taos. Captain Francisco de Barrionuevo also passed this way the following year on his way to the same pueblo.

Río Grande Gorge [46]

The Río Grande cut this spectacular gorge through layers of basalt, a volcanic rock that erupted between 2 and 5 million years ago. This basalt was highly fluid and flowed many miles. The enormous landslide blocks downstream were caused by undercutting when the river was much larger during the Pleistocene glacial age.

Pueblo Revolt Tricentennial [47]

The 1680 Pueblo Revolt began at the Pueblo of Taos when Popé, a religious leader driven from San Juan by Spanish authorities, sent runners carrying a knotted cord to other pueblos designating the number of days until the uprising. Tiwa warriors from Taos and Picurís moved south on August 10 to beseige Santa Fe.

Embudo Stream-Gaging Station [48]
Established in 1888

Site of the first United States Geological Survey training center for hydrographers. Those trained here made some of the earliest hydrological studies in the nation, leading to stream-gaging of many streams throughout the country, and thus providing important evaluations of the nation's surface water resources.

Cantonment Burgwin – 1852-1860 [49]

Never officially designated a fort, this post was built to protect the Taos Valley from Utes and Jicarilla Apaches. It is named for Capt. John H.K. Burgwin, who was killed in the Taos uprising of 1847. It was abandoned in 1860 and is now the site of the Fort Burgwin Research Center.

San Francisco de Asis Church
Ranchos de Taos, New Mexico [50]

This Mission Church is one of the oldest churches in America dedicated to San Francisco de Asis. It was constructed between 1813 and 1815 under the direction of the Franciscan Fray José Benito Pereyro. It is an outstanding example of adobe mission architecture. This Church continues to this day to be a place of worship and an integral part of the community.

Taos [51]
Population—3369   Elevation—6983 ft.

The Spanish community of Taos developed two miles southwest of Taos Pueblo. It later served as a supply base for the "Mountain Men," and was the home of Kit Carson, who is buried here. Governor Charles Bent was killed here in the anti-U.S. insurrection of 1847. In the early 1900s, Taos developed as a colony for artists and writers.

Taos Plaza
End of the Camino Real [52]

Spanish settlers lived in the Taos Valley before the Pueblo Revolt of 1680, but the town of Fernández de Taos was not founded until the 1790s. The Camino Real, or King's Highway, from Mexico City reached its end in this plaza and in nearby Taos Pueblo.

Kit Carson Memorial
State Park Cemetery [53]

In 1868, Christopher "Kit" Carson, the legendary guide, scout, soldier, and trapper, died in Fort Lyons, Colorado. The next year, his body and that of his wife Josefa were brought home to Taos. Others buried here include soldiers killed in the 1847 rebellion protesting the U.S. annexation of New Mexico.

Pueblo of Taos [54]

Parts of Taos were occupied when Hernando de Alvarado visited here in 1540. Taos served as the headquarters from which Popé, of San Juan Pueblo, organized the Pueblo Revolt in 1680. In 1846, the pueblo was a refuge for Hispanics and Indians resisting the annexation of New Mexico by the United States.

DAV Vietnam Veterans
National Memorial [55]

This Chapel was erected in 1968 by Dr. Victor Westphall in memory of his son and all other U.S. personnel killed in the fighting in Vietnam. It was first dedicated as the Vietnam Veterans Peace and Brotherhood Chapel, and on May 30, 1983, it was rededicated as the DAV Vietnam Veterans National Memorial.

Lawrence Ranch
University of New Mexico [56]

The Kiowa Ranch, home of novelist D.H. Lawrence and his wife Frieda in 1924-25, was given to them by Mabel Dodge Luhan. Frieda continued to live at the ranch after his death, and later married Angelo Ravagli. In 1934 they built a shrine for Lawrence's ashes. Aldous Huxley was among the many visitors to the ranch.

Palo Flechado Pass [57]
Elevation—9101 ft.

Palo Flechado (tree pierced with arrows) was a pass much used by Indians, Spaniards, and Anglos traveling from the plains by way of the Cimarron River (called La Flecha - the arrow - in 1719). The Flecha de Palo Indians (Apache band) in 1706 inhabited the plains east of the mountains.

Río Grande Rift [58]

A tremendous split in the earth's crust has resulted in the Río Grande rift basin filled with thousands of feet of alluvium from bordering mountains and lava flows from deep within the earth. About 650 feet of this basin-fill is exposed in the Río Grande Gorge at the bridge crossing.

Ojo Caliente [59]
Elevation—6294 ft.

Ojo Caliente ("hot spring" in Spanish) was a strategic point for the defense of the Chama and upper Río Grande Valleys. Colonization began in the early 18th century, but pressure from the Utes and Comanches delayed permanent settlement until 1793. In 1807, Lt. Zebulon Pike reported a population of 500.

Domínguez-Vélez de Escalante Trail [60]

In order to open a trail between Santa Fe and Monterey, California, and to spread Christianity among the Indians, Fray Francisco Atanasio Domínguez and Fray Silvestre Vélez de Escalante led a small party northwest in 1776. Abiquiú was the last Spanish settlement they saw in their five-month 2000-mile journey.

El Rito [61]

Elevation—6870 ft.

This village was settled in the 1830s by residents from the Abiquiú area. The Territorial Legislature of 1909 established the Spanish-American Normal School here to train teachers for northern New Mexico schools. After several changes in name and purpose, the institution is now the Northern New Mexico Community College.

Abiquiú [62]

Established on the site of an abandoned Indian pueblo, Abiquiú in the mid-18th century became a settlement of Spaniards and genízaros (Hispanicized Indians). In 1776, explorers Fray Francisco Atanacio Domínguez and Fray Silvestre Vélez de Escalante visited here. In 1830, the settlement became one of the stops on the Spanish Trail which linked Santa Fe with Los Angeles, California.

Red Rocks [63]

The colorful formations exposed here are the slope forming Chinle Shale of Triassic age deposited in streams, lakes and floodplains some 250 million years ago and the cliff forming Entrada Sandstone of Jurassic age deposited as windblown sand some 160 million years ago. These are typical landforms of the Colorado Plateau province.

Old Spanish Trail [64]

In 1829-30, Antonio Armijo traveled from Abiquiú to California to trade for mules, thus extending the Old Spanish Trail and opening it to trade between Santa Fe and Los Angeles. His route turned west, near present-day Abiquiú Dam, to Largo Canyon, which led him to the San Juan River.

Colorado Plateau [65]

From this point, the Colorado Plateau extends across northwestern New Mexico into northeastern Arizona, southeastern Utah, and southwestern Colorado. A colorful landscape of mesas, and canyons, it is underlain by natural mineral, oil, and gas resources locked within sedimentary strata deposited millions of years ago. Elevation 6,400 feet.

Brazos Cliffs [66]

These precipitous cliffs form the western edge of the Tusas Mountains, a Rocky Mountain highland that enters New Mexico from Colorado. They are composed of some of the oldest rock known in New Mexico, the Precambrian quartzite about 1.7 billion years old. Vertical distance from summit to base is more than 2,000 feet. Elevation here 10,000 feet.

Tierra Amarilla [67]

Elevation—7860 ft.

In 1832 the Mexican government made a large community land grant to Manuel Martínez and other settlers, but settlement was delayed by raids by Utes, Jicarilla Apaches and Navajos. Tierra Amarilla, first called Nutritas, became the Río Arriba County seat in 1880. In 1967 it was the focus of conflicts between National Guardsmen and land rights activist Reies López Tijerina.

Fort Lowell [68]

Fort Lowell was established in 1866 to protect the Tierra Amarilla area settlements from the Southern Utes. Originally named Camp Plummer, this post was garrisoned by a detachment of New Mexico Volunteers, some of whose descendents live in the area. The fort was abandoned in 1869 and its log, or "fuerte" buildings sold to local residents.

Chama [69]

Population—1090   Elevation—7860 ft.

From a small crossroads town, Chama became an important site on the Denver & Río Grande Western Railroad after 1880. The Cumbres & Toltec Scenic Railroad is the remnant of the San Juan Extension, a narrow-gauge line which once served the mining areas of southwestern Colorado.

Cumbres & Toltec Scenic Railroad [70]

In 1880-82 the Denver & Río Grande Railroad built the San Juan Extension to serve the mines of southwestern Colorado. The Cumbres & Toltec Scenic Railroad still operates 64 miles of the narrow-gauge system between Chama, N.M., and Antonito, Colorado. Jointly owned by the two states, it is a "living museum" of railway history.

Cumbres Pass [71]

A major encounter between the U.S. Army and a large group of Utes and Jicarilla Apaches occurred here in July 1848. Old Bill Williams, the famous scout and guide, was badly wounded while fighting the Utes, who had once adopted him as a tribesman.

PUEBLO OF TAOS 1939

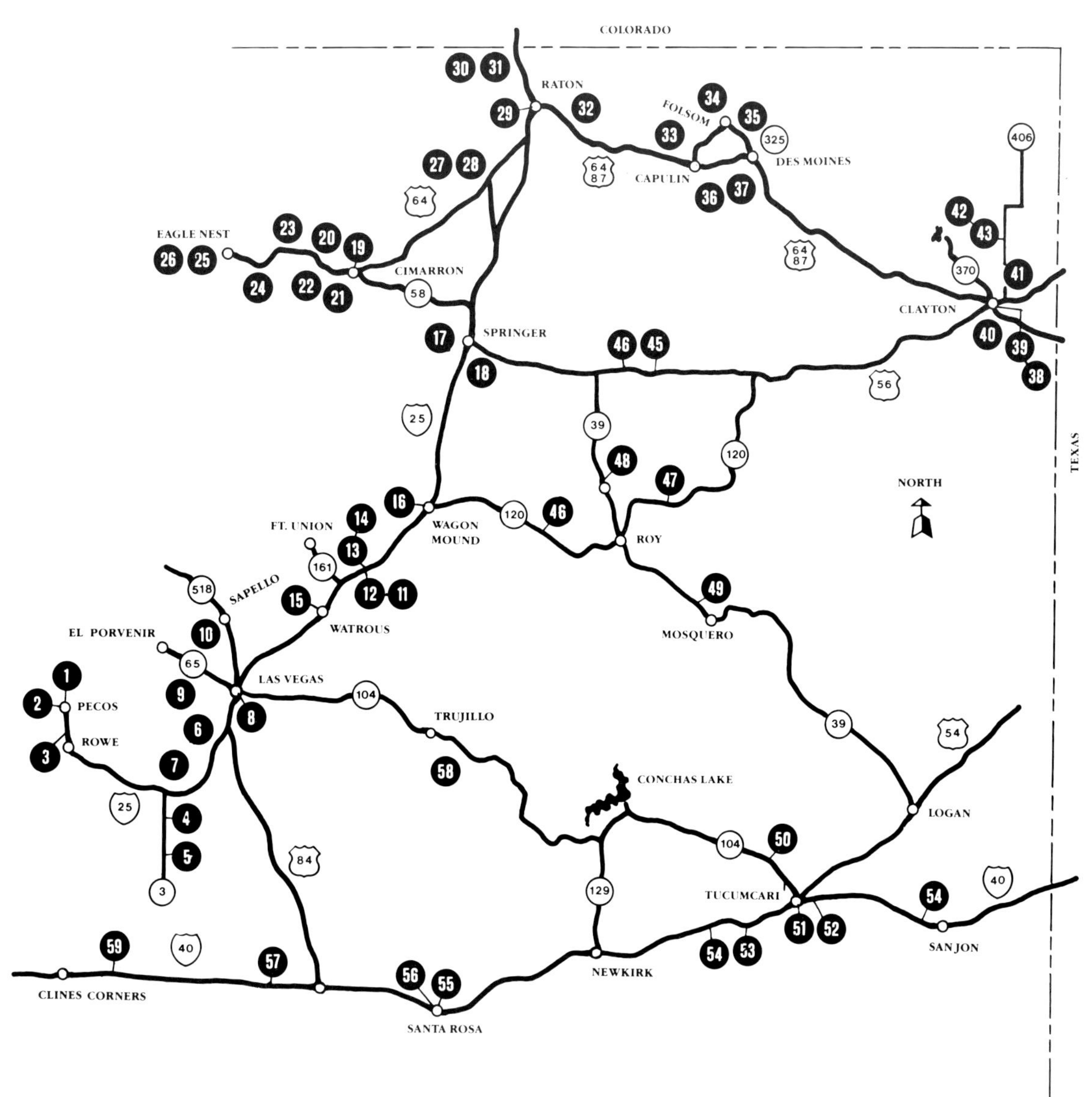

REGIONAL MAP NUMBER THREE

Map Symbols

Historical Markers . . . . **1**—**59**

Interstate Highways . . . .

U.S. Highways . . . .

State Highways . . . .

FORT UNION NATIONAL MONUMENT

Pecos [1]

The upper Pecos River Valley was on the frontier of Pueblo Indian civilization from at least the 13th to the 19th centuries, when the nearby Pueblo of Pecos was abandoned. Despite raids by various Plains Indian groups, Spanish-speaking settlers around 1825 founded what is today the village of Pecos.

San Antonio De Padua Catholic Church [2]

This is one of the finest surviving examples of Bishop Lamy's French-inspired gothic architecture in New Mexico. Completed in 1906, it is constructed of locally quarried stone instead of traditional adobe. Among its adornments is a painting of Nuestra Senora de Los Angeles (Our Lady of the Angles), given to the nearby Pueblo of Pecos by the King of Spain in the early eighteenth century.

Pecos National Monument [3]

In 1540-41, this pueblo stood 5 stories high and accommodated a population of 500. Four churches and an additional pueblo were built here in the 1600s and 1700s. Disease and Comanche raids in the late 1700s significantly reduced the size of the community. In 1838, the remaining 17 people moved to the Pueblo of Jémez.

The name Pecos is derived from the name given it by its Keres Indian neighbors, though the Towa-speaking inhabitants called it Cicuyé. Excavations in the early 1900s and 1940 provided much information on the history of the pueblo. It has been a National Monument since 1965.

Settlements Of The San Miguel Del Vado Land Grant [4]

Soon after the Spanish Government approved the San Miguel del Vado Land Grant in 1794, settlements such as San Miguel, Puertecito, San José, Las Mulas, Entranosa, Guzano, Bernal, La Cuesta and El Pueblo were established along the banks of the Pecos River. Others such as San Juan, Rivera, El Barranco, Sena, Lovato, La Fragua and El Cerrito were founded later in the 19th century.

Villanueva [5]

Originally named La Cuesta by its founders, this village was renamed Villanueva in the late 19th century. It was one of the earliest settlements established along the Pecos River when the San Miguel del Vado Land Grant was approved by the Spanish Government in 1794. The village church, completed by 1830, is an excellent example of 19th century New Mexico religious architecture.

Hermit's Peak [6]

Elevation — 10,212 ft.

From 1863 to 1867 this mountain was the home of Juan María Agostíni, an Italian penitent who lived there as a hermit, carving crucifixes and religious emblems which he traded for food. Leaving this area, he moved to the Organ Mountains, in southern New Mexico, where he was found murdered in 1869.

Hogbacks [7]

Interstate 25 cuts through dipping strata that form hogback ridges between the Great Plains and the south end of the Rocky Mountains. The Santa Fe Trail from here to Santa Fe, followed a natural valley eroded in less resistant strata between the mountains to the north and Glorieta Mesa to the south. Elevation 6,200 feet.

Las Vegas [8]

Population—14,322   Elevation—6470 ft.

Las Vegas served as an important stop on the Santa Fe Trail and later as a major railroad center. Here General Kearny announced the annexation of New Mexico by the U.S. in 1846. In 1862, during the Confederate occupation of Santa Fe, Las Vegas served as a Territorial capital. New Mexico Highlands University was established here in 1893.

Camp Maximiliano Luna [9]

The 200th Coast Artillery, Anti-Aircraft, formerly the 111th Cavalry of the New Mexico National Guard, trained here before going to the Philippines in World War II. About half of the men died either on the infamous Bataan Death March of 1942, or in Japanese prison camps afterwards.

Strike Valleys [10]

Between Sapello and Mora, State Road 3 follows a narrow strike valley eroded into soft shale between ridges of resistant sandstone called hogbacks, both the result of uplift of the Rocky Mountains. To the east stretch the Great Plains and to the west, the Sangre de Cristo Mountains rise to elevations exceeding 13,000 feet. Elevation here 7,000 feet.

Fort Union National Monument [11]
1851-1891

Once the largest post in the Southwest, Fort Union was established to control the Jicarilla Apaches and Utes, to protect the Santa Fe Trail, and to serve as a supply depot for other New Mexico forts. The arrival of the railroad and the pacification of the region led to its abandonment in 1891.

Santa Fe Trail [12]

Opened by William Becknell in 1821, the Santa Fe Trail became the major trade route to Santa Fe from Missouri River towns. The two main branches, the Cimarron Cutoff and the Mountain Branch, joined at Watrous. Travel over the Trail ceased with the coming of the railroad in 1879.

Tiptonville [13]

In 1862, William B. Tipton built his home one-half mile west of here. By 1870, he had laid out the town of Tiptonville along the banks of the Mora River. The town served as a stopover and meeting place for Santa Fe Trail travelers as well as soldiers from Fort Union. It boasted a mission school, Masonic Lodge, stores and a post office.

Fort Union Arsenal [14]

West of Fort Union near the base of the mesa are the ruins of Fort Union Arsenal. The first Fort Union was built at this location in 1851. In 1867 this wooden fort was razed and the adobe Arsenal erected. This Arsenal played a vital role in supplying armaments to military posts throughout New Mexico until 1882.

Watrous [15]

The Mountain Branch and the Cimarron Cutoff of the Santa Fe Trail meet at Watrous. This important spot on the Trail was first known as La Junta, "junction" in Spanish. In 1879, with the coming of the railroad, it was named for Samuel B. Watrous, a prominent local rancher.

Wagon Mound [16]

This last great landmark on the Santa Fe Trail was named for its resemblance to the top of a covered wagon. At Wagon Mound, travelers could cross from the Cimarron Cutoff to Fort Union, which is located on the Mountain Branch of the Trail. The two branches joined south of here at Watrous.

Springer [17]

Population—1696   Elevation—5857 ft.

Located in the old Maxwell Land Grant and near the Cimarron Cutoff of the Santa Fe Trail, Springer served as Colfax County seat from 1882 to 1897. Several men were killed here in one of the late flare-ups of the Colfax County War, a dispute between land grant owners and settlers.

Old Colfax County Courthouse [18]

Built in 1879 at a cost of $9,800, this building served as Colfax County Courthouse from 1882 through 1897, when the county seat was moved to Raton. This building housed the New Mexico reform school for boys from 1910 to 1917 and has been a public library, town hall and city jail.

Cimarron [19]

Population—888   Elevation—6427 ft.

This village on the Mountain Branch of the Santa Fe Trail was settled around 1844. In 1857 it became the home of Lucien B. Maxwell, and headquarters for the famous Maxwell Land Grant of almost 2,000,000 acres. An agency for Utes and Jicarilla Apaches was located here from 1862 to 1876.

Colfax County War [20]

For twenty years after the 1869 sale of the Maxwell Land Grant, homesteaders, ranchers, and miners fought the new owners for control of this enormous region. The resulting murders and general breakdown of law and order led to the removal from office, in 1878, of Territorial Governor Samuel B. Axtell.

Pueblo of Taos
No. 54, page 19
New Mexico State Tourist & Travel Division

Black Jack's Hideout [21]

In Turkey Creek Canyon near here, the outlaw gang of Thomas "Black Jack" Ketchum had one of its hideouts. After a train robbery in July 1899, a posse surprised the gang at the hideout. The outlaws scattered after a bloody battle, and the Ketchum gang was broken up.

Philmont Scout Ranch [22]

Oklahoma oilman Waite Phillips gave this 127,000 acre property to the Boy Scouts of America in 1938 and 1941. The first National Boy Scout Camp ever established, Philmont now hosts young men from all over the world. Kit Carson, Lucien B. Maxwell, and Dick Wootten were important in the history of the area.

Cimarron Canyon [23]

You are now at the Great Plains-Rocky Mountain boundary. The Cimarron Range is one of the easternmost ranges of the Sangre de Cristo Mountains in this part of New Mexico. Elevation 6,800 feet.

Palisades Sill [24]

These spectacular cliffs are cut by the Cimarron River through igneous rock known as a sill and composed of the rock type monzonite which was emplaced some 40 million years ago as these Southern Rocky Mountains were being uplifted. Elevation 8,000 feet.

Wheeler Peak [25]

Across Moreno Valley stands Wheeler Peak, 13,161 feet, highest peak in New Mexico. Rocks of Wheeler Peak and the Taos Range are highly resistant granites and gneisses of Precambrian age. Moreno Valley is underlain by soft sandstones and shales which are covered by stream and glacial deposits. Placer gold was mined at Elizabethtown north of here during the 1860's.

Elizabethtown [26]

The discovery of gold on Baldy Mountain in 1866 brought such a rush of fortune-seekers to the Moreno Valley that "E-town" became a roaring mining camp almost overnight. Because of water and transportation problems, and a decline in ore quality, it had become virtually a ghost town by 1875.

Santa Fe Trail [27]

William Becknell, the first Santa Fe Trail trader, entered Santa Fe in 1821 after Mexico became independent from Spain and opened its frontier to foreign traders. The Mountain Branch over Raton Pass divided here. One fork turned west to Cimarron, then south and joined a more direct route at Rayado.

The difficulty of bringing caravans over rocky and mountainous Raton Pass kept most wagon traffic on the Cimarron Cutoff of the Santa Fe Trail until the 1840s. Afterwards, the Mountain Branch, which here approaches Raton Pass, became more popular with traders, immigrants, gold-seekers, and government supply trains.

Clifton House Site [28]

Three-quarters of a mile west of here at the Canadian River crossing was the popular overnight stage stop on the Old Santa Fe Trail. Clifton House was built in 1867 by rancher Tom Stockton, and materials were brought here overland from Dodge City. For years it served as headquarters for cattle roundups. After abandonment of the Santa Fe Trail in 1879, it fell into disuse and burned.

Raton [29]

Population—8225   Elevation—6379 ft.

Once the Willow Springs freight stop on the Santa Fe Trail, the town of Raton developed from A.T. & S.F. repair shops established when the railroad crossed Raton Pass in 1879. Valuable coal deposits attracted early settlers. Nearby Clifton House was a stagecoach stop until the Trail was abandoned after 1879.

Raton Pass [30]

This important pass on the Mountain Branch of the Santa Fe Trail was used by Brigadier General Stephen Watts Kearny for his 1846 invasion of New Mexico, and by the Colorado Volunteers who defeated the Confederates in 1862. Richens L. "Uncle Dick" Wooten operated a toll road from 1866 to 1879, when the Santa Fe Railroad crossed the pass.

Willow Springs [31]

In 1861, the U.S. Army established a government forage station here by a small spring. A well was dug, and the station became a water stop for Barlow and Sanderson stagecoaches. With the arrival of the railroad in 1879 and the founding of Raton, the station was incorporated into the new town and eventually was razed.

Rocky Mountains [32]

The Sangre de Cristo ranges of the Southern Rocky Mountains visible here include the Spanish Peaks in Colorado, and the Culebra and Cimarron Ranges in New Mexico. Reaching altitudes of more than 13,000 feet, the well watered and forested mountains offer numerous recreational activities including skiing, hiking, fishing, hunting and climbing.

Capulin Mountain National Monument [33]

An outstanding example of an extinct volcanic cinder cone, Capulin Mountain was formed as early as 10,000 years ago. In cinder cones, lava pours from cracks in the base rather than over the top. Capulin itself was the escape hatch for gases that blew lava fragments into the air where they solidified and landed red hot on the cone.

Folsom Archaeological Site [34]

Near here was the site of the discovery of a spear point between the ribs of an extinct species of bison. This find established man's presence in North America about 10,000 years ago, prior to the extinction of large mammals at the end of the last Ice Age.

Tollgate Canyon [35]

Between 1871 and 1873, Bazil Metcalf constructed a toll road from the Dry Cimarron through Tollgate Gap, providing one of the few reliable wagon roads between Colorado and northeast New Mexico. This road remained an important commercial route until the Colorado and Southern Railway came through this area in the late 1880's.

Goodnight-Loving Trail [36]

In order to avoid the high toll charged for each animal on the Raton Pass branch of the Goodnight-Loving Trail, Charles Goodnight blazed this route through Trinchera Pass in 1868. Because it was shorter, had easier grades,and was toll-free, later cattle drives followed Goodnight's example.

Sierra Grande [37]

Largest extinct volcano in northeastern New Mexico, Sierra Grande rises to an elevation of 8,720 feet, one of many volcanoes, cinder cones, and flows that cover more than 1,000 square miles of area in northeastern New Mexico and southeastern Colorado eastward to the Oklahoma state line.

Clayton [38]

Population—2968   Elevation—4969 ft.

Trade caravans and homesteaders traveling the Cimarron Cutoff of the Santa Fe Trail passed near here. Clayton was founded in 1887 and named for the son of cattleman and ex-Senator Stephen W. Dorsey, one of its developers. It became a major livestock shipping center for herds from the Pecos Valley and the Texas Panhandle.

Clayton Dinosaur Trackway [39]

One of the best dinosaur track sites in the world can be viewed at Clayton Lake State Park. More than 500 fossilized footprints, made by at least eight kinds of dinosaurs, are visible on the lake's spillway. These tracks were embedded in the mud over 100 million years ago, when most of New Mexico was a vast sea.

Rabbit Ear Mountains [40]

These two striking mounds were the first features to become visible to Santa Fe Trail traffic crossing into New Mexico from Oklahoma, and so became important landmarks for caravans. From here, traffic on this major 19th-century commercial route still had about 200 miles to travel before reaching Santa Fe.

Black Jack Ketchum [41]

Thomas ''Black Jack'' Ketchum, leader of a notorious band of train robbers, was wounded in August 1899 while trying to rob a train near Folsom. He surrendered the next day. He was tried and convicted under a law making train robbery a capital offense, and hanged at Clayton on April 26, 1901.

McNees Crossing [42]

Here the Santa Fe Trail crossed the North Canadian River. The site is named for two young men, McNees and Monroe, who were shot at this crossing in 1828. Here too, a group of travelers celebrated Independence Day in 1831, the first documented 4th of July observation on the plains. Original trail ruts can still be seen near the crossing.

Santa Fe Trail Ruts [43]

From 1821 until the railroad arrived in New Mexico in 1879, thousands of wagons hauled freight along the Santa Fe Trail between Missouri and Santa Fe. These wagons carved ruts which have since eroded and deepened, creating a wide swath which is the only visible remains of the Trail. Ruts of the Mountain Branch of the Trail can be seen 1.2 miles ahead.

Point of Rocks [44]

Point of Rocks was a major landmark on the Santa Fe Trail. Located in Jicarilla Apache country, it was near here that the party of Santa Fe merchant J.W. White was attacked in 1849. Kit Carson was a member of the military party organized to rescue White's wife and daughter.

View of the Rockies [45]

Reaching altitudes of more than 13,000 feet, well watered, and forested, the Rocky Mountains are host to numerous recreational activities including skiing, fishing, hunting, and camping. To the north can be seen numerous volcanic peaks that lie east of the Rocky Mountains in both Colorado and New Mexico. Elevation here 6,300 feet.

Treeless grasslands of the High Plains cover the eastern one-third of New Mexico and stretch eastward into the mid-continent. Surface water from the mountains beyond and underground aquifers permit ranching as the principal economic activity. Carbon dioxide gas, a geologic resource, has been discovered and developed in the subsurface.

Canadian River Canyon [46]

Flowing out of the Rockies, the Canadian River has cut a gorge 600 feet deep through sedimentary strata of the High Plains. Rim elevation is 5,400 feet.

New Goodnight Trail [47]

Charles Goodnight, the great Texas cattleman, used the Trinchera Pass branch of the Goodnight-Loving Trail until 1875. In that year, he blazed this trail northward from Fort Sumner, passing near Tucumcari and Clayton. This was the last trail created by Goodnight, marking the end of his operations in New Mexico.

Mills Canyon [48]

The site of one of New Mexico's most spectacular horticultural enterprises, the Orchard Ranch, established by Melvin W. Mills of Springer and notable for its skillfully engineered irrigation system. The ranch cultivated 12 miles of land along the Canadian River. Vegetable gardens and several thousand fruit trees flourished in the 1880s and later. A destructive flood wiped out orchards, irrigation system, buildings, and other improvements in 1904. They were never replaced.

Goodnight-Loving Trail [49]

After leaving Fort Sumner, the Goodnight-Loving Trail forked in two directions. This branch, developed by Oliver Loving in 1866, followed the Pecos River to Las Vegas, and the Santa Fe Trail to Raton Pass. The great Texas cattle drives followed this and other routes to Colorado and Wyoming until 1880.

Fort Bascom — 1863-1870 [50]

Fort Bascom was built to protect this area from Comanches. In 1864, Kit Carson led a campaign against the Comanches, as did General Philip Sheridan in 1868. The fort was also established to control the *Comancheros,* New Mexicans involved in illegal trade with the Comanches. Fort Bascom was abandoned in 1870.

Tucumcari [51]

Population—6765   Elevation—4096 ft.
This area was troubled by both Comanches and *Comancheros,* New Mexicans who traded illegally with the Indians, until the military campaigns of 1874. With the coming of the railroad in 1898, the small community of Liberty, eight miles to the north, moved here to form the nucleus of Tucumcari, which was incorporated in 1908.

Tucumcari Mountain [52]

Tucumcari Mountain has long been a landmark for travelers along the Canadian River. Pedro Vial mentioned it in 1793, while opening a trail between Santa Fe and St. Louis. In order to find the best route from Arkansas to California, Capt. Randolph B. Marcy led an expedition past here in 1849.

Comanche Country [53]

By 1700 the Comanches had acquired the horse and began moving into this area. They drove out the Jicarilla Apaches, and their raids on New Mexico's eastern frontier posed a threat to Indian, Spanish, and Anglo settlements for over a century. The Comanches were finally defeated by the U.S. Army in 1874.

Llano Estacado [54]

Rising above these red-earth lowlands to the south is the Llano Estacado or Stockaded Plain, a high plateau covering some 32,000 square miles in eastern New Mexico and adjacent areas in Texas. Topographically, it is one of the flattest areas in the United States, and rises to 450 feet above the surrounding Great Plains.

Sediments shed from the rising mountains to the west formed the Llano Estacado, later to by bypassed by streams such as the Pecos and Canadian Rivers and left standing in bold relief with a relatively level, uneroded caprock surface. Croplands on the plain are irrigated using "fossil" water pumped from underground aquifers.

Santa Rosa [55]

Population—2469   Elevation—4620 ft.
The Spanish explorer Antonio de Espejo passed through this area in 1583, as did Gaspar Castaño de Sosa in 1590. Santa Rosa, the Guadalupe County seat, was laid out on the ranch of Celso Baca y Baca, a politician and rancher in the late 1800s. It was named for his wife, Doña Rosa.

Vasquez de Coronado's Route [56]

In 1540 Francisco Vasquez de Coronado and a small army set out from Mexico to search for the fabled Quivera and its cities of gold. In the spring of 1541, the expedition halted near here for four days while they built a log bridge across the Pecos River. From there they continued their exploration deep into present-day Kansas.

Trail of the Forty-Niners [57]

To give gold-seekers another route to California, Capt. Randolph B. Marcy and Lt. James H. Simpson opened a wagon road from Arkansas to New Mexico in 1849. Marcy's Road, although very popular with the Forty-Niners, still was never as well-traveled as the Santa Fe Trail. Here the route parallels I-40 to Albuquerque.

Canadian Escarpment [58]

This is a prominent landform of northeastern New Mexico that extends for almost 100 miles between Las Vegas and Clayton. From this point, the grasslands of the High Plains reach northwestward to the foot of the Southern Rocky Mountains which rise to elevations of more than 13,000 feet. Elevation here 6,300 feet.

Edge of Plains [59]

Grassy plains meet pine dotted uplands in this transition from Great Plains to Basin and Range provinces. Plains to the east are capped by caliche, sand, and gravel which are deeply eroded into underlying bedrock in places. To the west, faulting has produced alternating highlands and intermountain basins of the Basin and Range province. Elevation 6,500 feet.

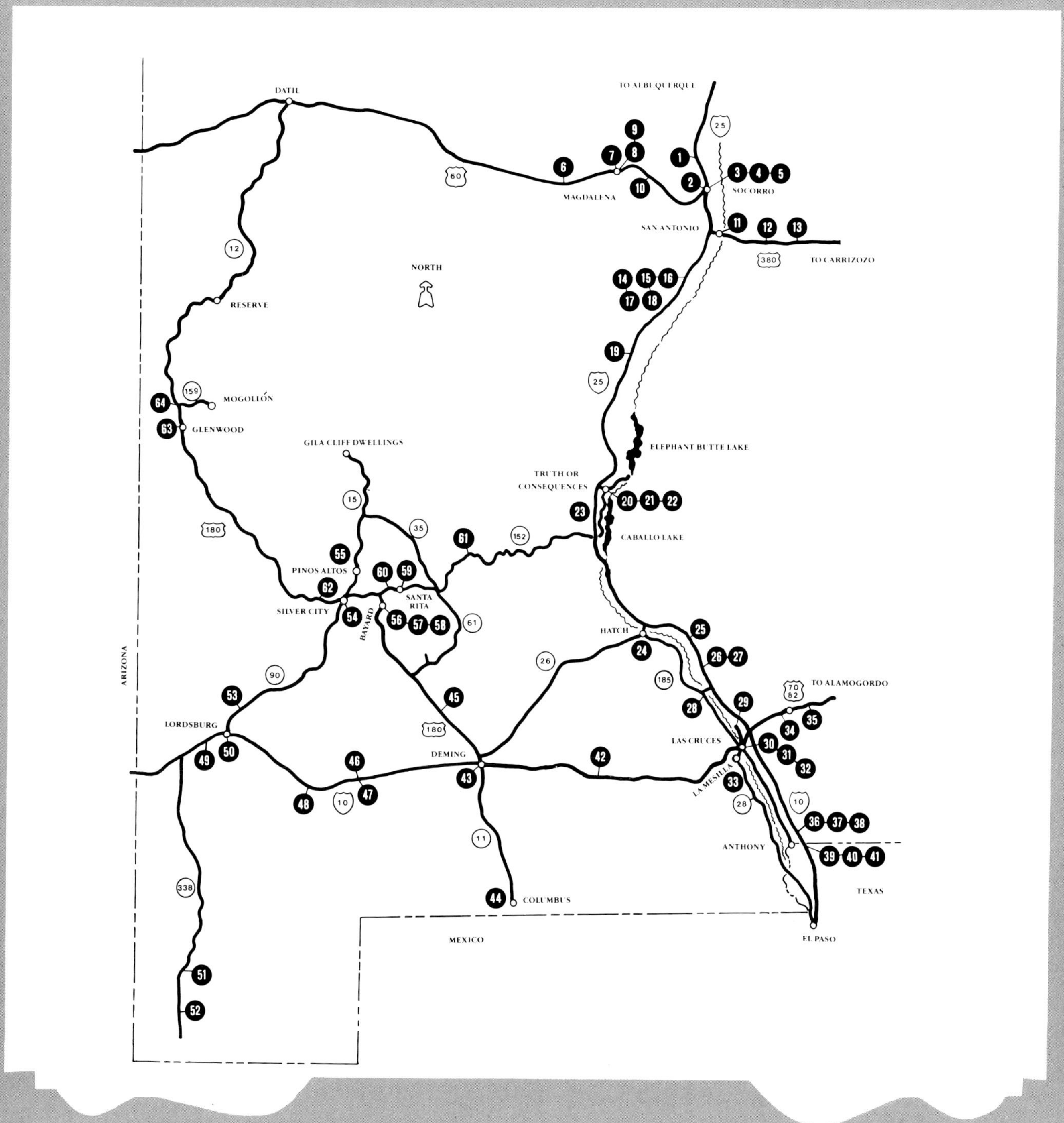

REGIONAL MAP NUMBER FOUR

Map Symbols

Historical Markers . . . . **1** — **64**

Interstate Highways . . . .

U.S. Highways . . . .

State Highways . . . .

4

Río Salado Sand Dunes [1]

Sand blown northeastward from normally dry bed of Río Salado forms dunes along this part of Río Grande Valley. Río Grande is in deep down-dropped trench with uplifted Los Pinos Mountains to east and Ladrón Mountains to northwest. Rocks on crest of Ladrons are 4 miles deep below sand dunes. Elevation 4,850 feet.

Socorro [2]

Population—7576   Elevation—4618 ft.

First seen by the Spanish in 1581 and visited by Juan de Oñate in 1598. Piro-speaking Pueblo Indians reportedly supplied much-needed corn, hence the name Socorro (help in Spanish). The Church of Nuestra Señora de Pilabó del Socorro was built about 1629. Abandoned in the Pueblo Revolt of 1680, the present town was founded in 1816.

Socorro Plaza Kittrell Park [3]

Established in 1816 at the time of the original Spanish land grant, this plaza developed into the traditional social, political and economic hub of the community. Excellent examples of Mexican and Territorial period architecture surround the plaza, which is named after Dr. L.E. Kittrell, a local dentist who landscaped the plaza in the 1880's.

New Mexico Tech [4]

The New Mexico School of Mines was established in 1889 to train engineers and technicians for the Territory's developing mining industry. The school opened its doors in September 1893 with 7 students. Now known as the New Mexico Institute of Mining and Technology, Tech offers degrees including the doctorate in a number of science and engineering disciplines.

New Mexico Bureau of Mines and Mineral Resources Museum [5]

Based on the personal collection willed to the New Mexico School of Mines by C.T. Brown in 1928, this museum displays thousands of mineral specimens from around the world with special emphasis on minerals found in New Mexico. Highlights include smithsonite from Kelly (Magdalena District), linarite from Bingham, Grants District uranium, Carlsbad potash, Silver City copper, Harding pegmatite minerals, and numerous fossils.

Plains of San Agustín [6]

Northeast part of Plains of San Agustín, occupied some thousands of years ago by large intermontane lake, is downdropped graben bordered by uplifted volcanic masses. San Mateo and Luera Mountains and Pelona Mountain are southeast and Horse Mountain and Datil Mountains are northwest. Elevation 7,030 feet.

Magdalena [7]

Magdalena is located in a mineral-rich area which became a center of silver mining in the 1860s. In 1885, a railroad was built to the smelter in Socorro, and Magdalena became an important railhead for cattle, sheep, and ore.

Kelly [8]

Kelly was central New Mexico's most prosperous mining town from the 1880's until the early 20th century. Silver had been mined at Kelly since the 1860's, but in 1903, it became a major source of zinc carbonate, a vital ingredient in the manufacture of paint. Located 3.5 miles south of Magdalena on NM 114, Kelly is now a ghost town, but former residents still host a festival every October.

Riley [9]

Located twenty minutes north of Magdalena, Riley was a small agricultural village originally named Santa Rita by its Hispanic founders in the mid nineteenth century. During the late 1880's mining became an important part of the town's economy, but when the mines gave out, the town was slowly abandoned. Former residents still gather every May to observe Santa Rita days.

Magdalena Fault [10]

Magdalena Mountains to west are topped by South Baldy at 10,783 feet; La Jencia plain to east is down dropped with rocks in Water Canyon 3 miles below this sign. Bench along edge of mountains is Magdalena fault dividing uplifted mountains from downdropped plains. Elevation 6,110 feet.

San Antonio - On the Camino Real [11]

In the mid-19th century, San Antonio was the last outpost on the Camino Real before the Mesilla Valley to the south. Today it is known as the birthplace of Conrad Hilton and the site of the first Hilton Hotel, located in his family's adobe house near the train station.

Carthage-Tokay-Farley [12]

Important coal-mining towns from the 1880s to 1925 when the mines closed. Originally developed by the Santa Fe Railroad and later operated by the Carthage Fuel Company mainly to fire the Kinney brick kilns in Albuquerque. Farley was a limestone quarry. The Hilton Mine belonged to the father of Conrad Hilton.

Trinity Site [13]

The world's first atomic explosion occurred on July 16, 1945, at the Trinity Site near the north end of the historic Jornada del Muerto. It marked the beginning of the nuclear age, and the culmination of the Manhattan Project. The site, now part of the White Sands Missile Range, is closed to the public.

Valverde Battlefield [14]

The first major battle of the Civil War on New Mexico soil occurred at Valverde on February 21, 1862, when a Confederate force of Texas Volunteers under General H.H. Sibley defeated Union forces commanded by Col. E.R.S. Canby stationed at Fort Craig. From here, Sibley marched north and was defeated in Glorieta Pass near Santa Fe.

Mesa del Contadero [15]

The Chihuahua Trail passed by the large volcanic mesa on the east bank of the Río Grande, marking the northern end of the Jornada del Muerto (Journey of the Dead Man). "Contadero" means "the counting place," or a narrow place where people and animals must pass through one-by-one.

Fort Craig [16]

Fort Craig, which replaced Fort Conrad located about nine miles north, was established to control Indian raids along the Jornada del Muerto. Troops from Fort Craig were defeated by Confederate forces at the Battle of Valverde, 7 miles distant, in 1862. Capt. Jack Crawford, the "Poet-Scout," was stationed here.

Fort Craig Rest Area [17]

Fort Craig is on alluvial gravelly sands, derived from mountains to west, sloping toward Río Grande to east. Magdalena Mountains to northwest and San Mateo Mountains to west are mainly thick piles of volcanic rocks. San Andrés Mountains on southeast horizon are of older limestones and shales. Elevation 4,810 feet.

Espejo's Expedition On the Camino Real [18]

In 1582 and 1583, Antonio de Espejo and his party paralleled the Río Grande north to the Bernalillo area. He was trying to learn the fate of two Franciscan friars who had stayed with the Pueblo Indians after the Rodríguez-Sánchez Chamuscado expedition returned to Mexico in 1581.

ELEPHANT BUTTE DAM

Vásquez de Coronado's Route [19]

In 1541 an expedition from the army of Francisco Vásquez de Coronado, New Mexico's first explorer, marched south 80 leagues to investigate the pueblos along the lower Río Grande. The group reached that part of the infamous Jornada del Muerto, now covered by Elephant Butte Lake, where the river disappeared underground.

Elephant Butte Dam [20]

Pueblo Indians had been irrigating and farming in the Río Grande Valley for several hundred years before the Spaniards arrived to continue the tradition. The construction of Elephant Butte Dam, 1912-1916, represented the first large scale attempt to harness and control the river, and assured irrigation downstream.

Truth or Consequences [21]

Population—5219   Elevation—4576 ft.

In 1581, Capitan Francisco Sánchez Chamuscado took possession of this region for the King of Spain, naming it the Province of San Felipe. Significant European settlement of the area, however, did not occur until the mid-1800s. Once called Hot Springs because of its curative natural hot springs, "T or C" in 1950 took its present name from Ralph Edwards' radio program.

Gerónimo's Spring [22]

The Indians knew of the great curative powers of the mineral waters of this spring long before the white man came. According to legend, Geronimo, famous Apache war chief, often stopped here to bathe and relax.

Caballo Mountains [23]

To east beyond Caballo Reservoir are rugged Caballo Mountains, uplifted about 3 miles above downdropped Río Grande trough, along fault scarp at edge of mountains. Lowest slopes are ancient granites. Black ironstone beds are at base of high cliffs which are formed by Paleozoic dolomites and limestones. Elevation 4,390 feet.

Hatch [24]

Population—1028   Elevation—4055 ft.

Originally established as Santa Barbara in 1851, Apache raids drove the settlers away until 1853 when nearby Fort Thorn was established. Abandoned again in 1860 after the fort closed, it was re-occupied in 1875 and re-named for General Edward Hatch, then Commander of the New Mexico Military District.

Mormon Battalion [25]

The Mormon Battalion, composed of 500 volunteers, left Council Bluffs, Iowa, June 5, 1846, as part of the expeditionary force of Brigadier General Kearny. The battalion followed the Santa Fe Trail to Santa Fe and down the Río Grande near here, where it turned west. The 2000 mile march ended in San Diego, California, January 30, 1847.

Jornada del Muerto On the Camino Real [26]

This stretch of the Camino Real leaves the Río Grande and cuts across 90 miles of desert with little water or shelter. Despite its difficulty, the dreaded "Journey of the Deadman" was heavily used by Spanish, Mexican, and Anglo travelers between El Paso and the northern New Mexico settlements.

Jornada del Muerto [27]

High plains of Jornada del Muerto, elevation 4,340 feet, lie 400 feet above Río Grande Valley. Transitional area from Basin and Range region to west into tilted mountain ranges, such as San Andrés Mountains to east, flanked by broad alluvial and wind-blown basins, such as Jornada del Muerto.

Fort Selden State Monument [28]
1865-1891

Fort Selden was established to protect settlers and railroad construction crews in the Mesilla Valley and the Jornada del Muerto from Apaches. The first regular army troops to garrison it were four companies of the black 125th Infantry. General Douglas MacArthur spent two years of his childhood here. The fort was finally abandoned in 1891.

Bartlett-García Conde [29]
Initial Survey Point

On April 24, 1851, John Russell Bartlett, for the United States, and Pedro García Conde, for the Republic of Mexico, erected near here a monument designating 32°22' north latitude on the Río Grande as the initial point for the official survey of the U.S.-Mexico boundary. After the Gadsden Purchase, the boundary was moved south.

Las Cruces – On the Camino Real [30]

Population—46,086   Elevation—3909 ft.

In 1849, following the Mexican War, fields were first broken in Las Cruces. The town became a flourishing stop on the Camino Real, deriving its name, "The Crosses," from the marking of graves of victims of an Apache attack. Las Cruces since 1881 has been the county seat of Doña Ana County.

La Mesilla [31]

After the Treaty of Guadalupe Hidalgo, which concluded the Mexican War in 1848, the Mexican government commissioned *Cura* Ramón Ortiz to settle Mesilla. He brought families from New Mexico and from Paso del Norte (modern Ciudad Juárez) to populate the Mesilla Civil Colony Grant, which by 1850 had over 800 inhabitants.

Organ Mountains [32]

Spectacular Organ Mountains to east tower over water-rich Río Grande Valley. High sharp peaks and massive cliffs of igneous rocks are part of ancient volcanos. Copper, silver, gold, lead and zinc were mined from Organ Mining District at north end of mountains. Basin and Range country is to west. Elevation 4,190 feet.

La Mesilla [33]

On November 16, 1854, a detachment from nearby Fort Fillmore raised the U.S. flag here confirming the Gadsden Purchase; thus the Gadsden territory was officially recognized as part of the United States. In 1858, the Butterfield stage began its run through Mesilla. During the Civil War, Mesilla was the capital of the Confederate Arizona Territory.

Site of San Agustín Springs [34]

Here on July 27, 1861, less than 300 Confederate troops intercepted 500 Union soldiers retreating from Fort Fillmore to Fort Stanton. Exhausted from the heat and famished for water, the Union troops straggled across the desert in a five-mile evacuation train. Unable to fight, Major Isaac Lynde surrendered his command without firing a single shot.

San Augustín Pass [35]

Divide between Tularosa Basin to east and Jornada del Muerto to west, cut between Organ Mountains to south and San Augustín-San Andrés Mountains to north. White gypsum sands glisten to northeast. Roadcuts in Tertiary monzonite. Organ mines yielded copper, lead, silver, gold, zinc and fluorite. Elevation 5,710 feet.

Ruins of Fort Selden

Brazito Battlefield [36]

One of the few battles of the Mexican War to be fought in New Mexico occurred near here on Christmas Day, 1846. U.S. troops under Colonel Alexander W. Doniphan defeated a Mexican army commanded by General Antonio Ponce de León. Two days later, Doniphan entered El Paso without opposition.

Espejo's Expedition – On the Camino Real [37]

Trying to locate two Franciscan friars, Antonio de Espejo in 1582 led an expedition up the Río Grande near here. The two friars had remained among the Tiwa Indians near Bernalillo after the Rodríguez-Sánchez Chamuscado expedition returned to Mexico in 1581. When he reached the Tiwas in 1583, Espejo learned that the missionaries were dead.

Butterfield Trail [38]

Stagecoaches of the Butterfield Overland Mail Co. began carrying passengers and mail from St. Louis to San Francisco, across southern New Mexico, in 1858. The 2,795-mile journey took 21-22 days. In 1861 the service was re-routed through Salt Lake City. Here the trail followed the Río Grande northward to La Mesilla.

Oñate's Route   On the Camino Real [39]

Juan de Oñate, first governor of New Mexico, passed near here with his colonizing expedition in May 1598. Traveling north, he designated official campsites (called *parajes*) on the Camino Real, used by expeditions that followed. In Oñate's caravan were 129 men, many with their families and servants.

El Camino Real (The King's Highway) [40]

The oldest historical road in the United States, running over 2000 miles from Mexico City to Taos. Parts of the Camino Real were used by Spanish explorers in the 1580s, but it was formally established in 1598 by Juan de Oñate, New Mexico's first colonizer and governor. It was later referred to as the Chihuahua Trail.

Franklin Mountains [41]

Franklin Mountains to east are tilted uplifted block of Paleozoic limestones. Spectacular Organ Mountains to north are mainly igneous rocks, mineralized in places. Paleozoic rocks encountered in oil tests to northwest in the Río Grande trench are 5 miles lower than in mountains, illustrating the Basin and Range geologic structure. Elevation 3,950 feet.

Fort Cummings—1863-1886 [42]

This small and isolated post was built on the Mesilla-Tucson road to protect the Butterfield Trail against Apaches. Notorious Cooke's Canyon, located nearby, was a particularly dangerous point on the trail. Only ruins now remain of the ten-foot adobe walls which once surrounded it.

Deming [43]

Population—9964   Elevation—4331 ft.

In 1780, Governor Juan Bautista de Anza passed near here while searching for a trade route between Santa Fe and the mines of Sonora, Mexico. Deming was founded in 1881 when the Santa Fe and Southern Pacific Railroads were connected, giving New Mexico its first railway access to both the Atlantic and the Pacific.

Pancho Villa's Raid [44]

On March 9, 1916, Francisco "Pancho" Villa, a major figure in the Mexican Revolution, crossed the international border with a large force, attacking and looting Columbus, New Mexico. Eighteen U.S. soldiers and civilians, and approximately 100 Villistas were killed. Gen. John J. "Black Jack" Pershing led an expeditionary force into Mexico in pursuit of Villa.

Butterfield Trail [45]

Stagecoaches of the Butterfield Overland Mail Co. began carrying passengers and mail from St. Louis to San Francisco, across southern New Mexico, in 1858. The 2,795-mile journey took 21-22 days. In 1861 the service was re-routed through Salt Lake City. From La Mesilla west, the trail paralleled I-10.

Basin and Range Country [46]

Basin and Range province of southwestern New Mexico consists of broad alluvial plains from which isolated fault block mountains rise like islands from a sandy sea. Victorio Mountains to south have yielded zinc, silver, gold, copper, lead, and tungsten to early miners and limestone for highway construction. Elevation 4,500 feet.

Cooke's Wagon Road [47]

In 1846, while leading the Mormon Battalion to California during the Mexican War, Lt. Col. Philip St. George Cooke blazed the first wagon road from New Mexico to the West Coast. The potential of the route for railroad construction was one of the reasons for the Gadsden Purchase in 1854. Cooke entered Arizona through Guadalupe Pass.

Yucca Plains [48]

Wide alluvial plains of southwestern New Mexico are feature of Basin and Range province with isolated fault block mountains scattered like islands from a sandy sea. Volcanic rocks form most of Cedar Mountains to south and Pyramid Mountains to west but Burro Mountains to northwest are mainly ancient granites. Elevation 4,560 feet.

Shakespeare [49]

After a silver strike in 1869, a townsite was laid out at the old stage stop of Mexican Springs. Named Ralston City, a diamond swindle caused its collapse in 1874. The town was revived as Shakespeare in 1879, but the depression of 1893 closed the mines and made it a ghost town.

SHAKESPEARE

Lordsburg [50]

Population—3195   Elevation—4245 ft.

Lordsburg was founded in 1880 on the route of the Southern Pacific Railroad, near that used by the Butterfield Overland Mail Co., 1858-1861. It eventually absorbed most of the population of Shakespeare, a now-deserted mining town three miles south.

Smugglers' Trail [51]

Smugglers once crossed this area with mule trains of contraband from Mexico, to be traded for merchandise in Arizona. In the summer of 1881, a group of Mexican smugglers was killed in Skeleton Canyon by members of the Clanton gang, including Old Man Clanton, Ike and Billy Clanton, and Curly Bill.

The Clanton Hideout [52]

The infamous Clanton Gang had two crude dugouts here in the 1880s that served as hideouts and a base for wide-ranging outlaw activities, particularly in connection with the Curly Bill Gang's depredations along the Smuggler's Trail that passed by here. Old Man Clanton was ambushed below the border in revenge for a Skeleton Canyon massacre.

McComas Incident [53]

In March 1883, Judge and Mrs. H.C. McComas were killed in this vicinity by a group of Chiricahua Apaches led by Chatto. An extensive manhunt failed to rescue their six-year-old son, who had been taken captive. This incident was part of a violent outbreak toward the end of the Apache wars.

Silver City [54]

Population—9887   Elevation—5895 ft.

Silver City is located in the midst of rich mineral deposits. The Santa Rita Copper Mines, opened in 1805, were the second such mines operating in what is now the U.S. A silver strike in 1870 began the commercial mining for which the area is still known. The Apache chiefs Victorio, Geronimo, and Mangas Coloradas figure in its history.

Pinos Altos [55]

In this area are extensive gold, silver and copper deposits mined as early as 1803. A new gold discovery in 1860 by three 49ers from California stimulated a boom that led to the establishment of the mining camp of Pinos Altos.

Once the Grant County seat, the town survived early Apache attacks to produce over $8,000,000 of gold, silver, copper, lead, and zinc before the mines played out in the 20th century.

Bayard [56]

Population—3036   Elevation—6152 ft.

Sites in the surrounding hills indicate that Indians of the Mogollon culture (A.D. 300-1450) lived here long before the Europeans. In the late 19th century, this was a stronghold of Apaches led by Victorio and Geronimo. Today Bayard, which was incorporated in 1925, lies in a great commercial mining region.

Fort Bayard—1866-1900 [57]

One of the several posts created on the Apache frontier, Fort Bayard protected the Pinos Altos mining district. Company B of the black 125th Infantry served here, as did Lt. John J. Pershing. In 1900 the fort became a military hospital, and today serves as Fort Bayard Medical Center.

Fort Bayard National Cemetery [58]

Originally established in 1866 as the military cemetery for Fort Bayard, many troopers, veterans, and civilians are buried here. It became a national cemetery, one of two in New Mexico, in 1973.

Santa Rita Copper Mines [59]

Copper has been mined here since 1804. For five years, development by Francisco Manuel Elguea resulted in some 6,000,000 pounds of copper being transported annually to Mexico City by mule train. Brief periods of activity were halted by Apache opposition until the coming of the railroad in the 1880s, when the area became a major copper producer.

Kneeling Nun [60]

Most famous of the many historic landmarks in the Black Range country is the Kneeling Nun. So named for its resemblance to a nun kneeling in prayer before a great altar. Many legends have grown up around the giant monolith which rests near the summit of the Santa Rita Range.

Emory Pass [61]

You are at crest of Black Range, elevation 8,828 feet, uplifted range of Tertiary volcanic and Paleozoic sedimentary rocks bordering Río Grande graben in which rock layers are about 4 miles lower than at pass. Same rocks cap Caballo Mountains, seen 35 miles to east on east side of Río Grande trough.

Mangas Coloradas [62]

Mangas Coloradas (Spanish for Red Sleeves) was a chief of the Mimbreño Apaches, who derived their name from the nearby Mimbres Mountains. Mangas Coloradas, a contemporary of legendary Apache chiefs Victorio and Cochise, led his people during the 1850s until he was captured near Pinos Altos in 1863. He was killed the night of January 18, 1863, while being held prisoner at Fort McLane, near present-day Hurley.

The Catwalk [63]

This steel causeway follows two pipelines which supplied water and water power to the old town of Graham where gold and silver ores were milled from nearby mines in the 1890s. The causeway clings to the sides of a sheer box canyon in Whitewater Creek and is accessible by a foot trail from the Whitewater picnic ground.

Mogollón [64]

The mountains and the town were named for Juan Ignacio Flores Mogollón, governor of New Mexico from 1712 to 1715. The name also is applied to the Pueblo Indians who abandoned the area in the early 1400s. These mountains were inhabited by Apaches until the late 19th century.

MOGOLLON GHOST TOWN

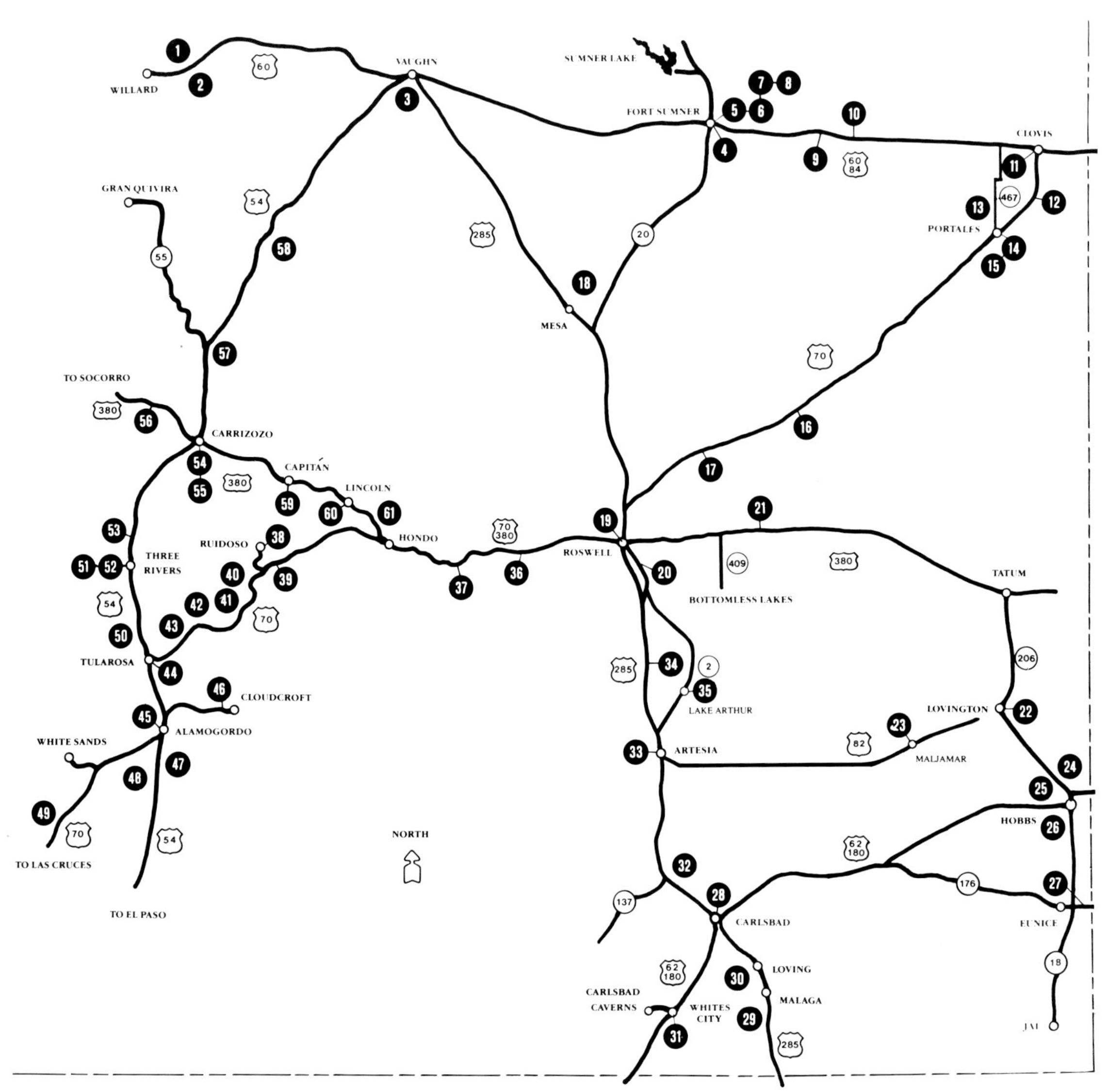

WILLARD
VAUGHN
SUMNER LAKE
FORT SUMNER
CLOVIS
GRAN QUIVIRA
PORTALES
MESA
TO SOCORRO
CARRIZOZO
CAPITÁN
LINCOLN
HONDO
ROSWELL
TATUM
RUIDOSO
THREE RIVERS
BOTTOMLESS LAKES
TULAROSA
LAKE ARTHUR
LOVINGTON
CLOUDCROFT
MALJAMAR
WHITE SANDS
ALAMOGORDO
ARTESIA
NORTH
HOBBS
TO LAS CRUCES
CARLSBAD
EUNICE
TO EL PASO
CARLSBAD CAVERNS
LOVING
MALAGA
WHITES CITY
JAL
60
54
55
285
20
60 84
467
70
380
380
55
54
380
70 380
409
380
285
2
206
82
54
70
62 180
137
176
18
62 180
285

REGIONAL MAP NUMBER FIVE
Map Symbols
Historical Markers
Interstate Highways
U.S. Highways
State Highways
5
1 51

Laguna Del Perro [1]

Numerous salt ponds and lakes, of which Laguna del Perro is the largest, occur in lowest part of Estancia Basin, closed depression between Manzano Mountains to west and low Pedernal Hills to east. Even paleoindians mined salt. Basin was filled by 150-foot-deep lake in late Pleistocene time. Elevation 6,110 feet.

Salt Lakes [2]

The Pedernal Hills form the eastern edge of Spanish New Mexico's 17th-century "Salinas Jurisdiction." Pueblo Indians used salt from these *salinas* in trade with Plains Indians. This salt was also prized by the Spaniards because of its use in silver processing for the rich Chihuahuan mines farther south in Mexico.

Vaughn [3]

Population—737   Elevation—5965 ft.

Vaughn, a division point in the transcontinental railway system, is located along the route of the Stinson cattle trail. In 1882, Jim Stinson, manager of the New Mexico Land and Livestock Co., drove 20,000 cattle in eight separate herds along this important trail from Texas to the Estancia Valley.

Fort Sumner [4]

Population—1421   Elevation—4028 ft.

Named for the fort built in 1862 to guard the Bosque Redondo Indian Reservation, the town of Fort Sumner grew out of settlements clustering around the Maxwell family properties. It moved to its present site with the construction of the Belén Cutoff of the Santa Fe Railroad around 1907.

Early Spanish Route [5]

In 1582, Antonio de Espejo and his exploring party left New Mexico to return to Mexico by way of the Pecos River. Eight years later, Gaspar Castaño de Sosa led another group into New Mexico alongside the same river, a route little used again until the Territorial period.

Fort Sumner State Monument
Old Fort Sumner and Bosque
Redondo Reservation—1862-1868 [6]

Fort Sumner was built to guard captive Indians confined to the Bosque Redondo Reservation. About 8000 were Navajos relocated from Arizona but there were also over 400 Mescalero Apaches. The fort was abandoned in 1868 when the Indians were allowed to return home. Lucien B. Maxwell and Billy the Kid figure in its later history.

Old Fort Sumner and
"Billy The Kid's" Grave [7]

Fort Sumner was established in 1862 to guard the Navajo and Apaches on the Bosque Redondo Reservation. It was discontinued as a military post in 1868 and the buildings and site sold to Lucien B. Maxwell. William "Billy the Kid' Bonney was killed here by Sheriff Pat Garrett the night of July 14, 1881. Bonney is buried in the nearby cemetery.

Sunnyside Springs [8]

Nearby is a "sweet water" spring which has been used through the centuries by Plains Indians, Spanish Explorers, and most recently, ranchers and settlers. A stagecoach station was located at the spring, which was named·after Sunnyside, the nearby settlement whose name was changed to Fort Sumner in 1910.

Stinking Springs [9]

William "Billy the Kid" Bonney and three members of his gang surrendered to a posse led by Sheriff Pat Garrett at a rock house near here on December 24, 1880. A fifth outlaw was killed during the gunfight. Bonney later escaped but was finally killed by Sheriff Garrett at Fort Sumner on July 14, 1881.

Llano Estacado [10]

Nomadic Indians and countless buffalo herds dominated this vast plain when the Vásquez de Coronado expedition explored it in 1541. Later it was the focus of Comanchero activity, and in the 19th century it became a center for cattle ranching. The name Llano Estacado, or stockaded plains, refers to the fortress-like appearance of its escarpments.

Clovis [11]

Population—31,194   Elevation—4260 ft.

During the 1700s and early 1800s, Comanche Indian buffalo hunters used trails that passed near here. In 1907 the Santa Fe Railroad established Clovis to serve as·the eastern terminal of the Belén Cutoff, which would connect with the transcontinental line at Belén. Formerly the domain of ranchers, the railroad opened the area to farmers.

Blackwater Draw [12]

In Blackwater Draw stream gravels are famous camp sites of Folsom Man. Draw is in Portales Valley, eroded into High Plains, and headwaters of Brazos River, beheaded by lower Pecos River in Pleistocene time. Local sand dunes conceal underlying Ogalalla sandstones whose "fossil" water feeds irrigated crops. Elevation 4,070 feet.

Los Portales Portales Springs [13]

Nearby is Los Portales, the site of a fresh water spring located among overhanging natural formations which according to Hispanic folklore reminded Spanish explorers of porches. During the late 19th century, this spring became an important stopping place along the trail between Fort Sumner and west Texas. William "Billy the Kid" Bonney and other outlaws frequently used the spring as a hideout.

Portales [14]

Population—9940   Elevation—4004 ft.

Portales derives its name from the porch-like appearance of a cave entrance at nearby Portales Springs. It developed as a major peanut producing region in the early twentieth century, after the Pecos Valley Railroad opened the area for commercial agricultural development. Eastern New Mexico University was founded here in 1934.

Eastern New Mexico University [15]

This University was established at Portales in 1927 by the State Legislature as the Eastern New Mexico Normal School. It opened for the 1934-35 school year with 274 students. Originally established to train teachers for rural schools, Eastern now has a wide range of undergraduate and graduate programs to serve the instructional, public service and research needs of the state and the nation.

Pecos Valley [16]

You are on plain bordering east side of Pecos Valley. Caprock escarpment, or west edge of Llano Estacado (Stockaded Plain) 15 miles to southwest on horizon. Capitán Mountains and Sierra Blanca on western skyline are east edge of Basin and Range province. Railroad Mountain, low east-west ridge 5 miles to south is igneous dike. Elevation 4,110 feet.

Castaño de Sosa's Route [17]

In 1590-91 Gaspar Castaño de Sosa, a Portuguese by birth, took an expedition up the Pecos River in an attempt to establish a colony in New Mexico. His venture was a failure, but it led to a permanent settlement under Don Juan de Oñate in 1598. Castaño de Sosa passed near here in the winter of 1590.

Mesa and Pecos Valley [18]

Pecos Valley section of Great Plains province stretches westward to foothills of Capitán, Jicarilla, and Gallinas Mountains. Southern High Plains, 50 miles to east, are capped by water-bearing Ogalalla Formation; Poquita Mesa to east is Ogalalla remnant. Nearby depressions are sinkholes in porous Permian limestones. Elevation 4,500 feet.

Roswell [19]

Population—39,676   Elevation—3612 ft.

Roswell was a watering place for the Pecos Valley cattle drives of the 1870s and 1880s. It was incorporated in 1891 and is seat of Chaves County, named for Col. J. Francisco Chaves, Civil War soldier and delegate to the U.S. Congress from the Territory of New Mexico. In the 1930s, Dr. Robert Goddard conducted experiments in liquid fuel rocket flights here.

Chisum's South Spring Ranch [20]

In 1875, John S. Chisum, the "Cattle King of the Pecos," made this the headquarters of a cattle ranching empire which extended for 150 miles along the Pecos River. In that year, 80,000 cattle bore his famous Jinglebob earmark. After Chisum's death, the ranch was acquired by J.J. Hagerman.

Goodnight-Loving Trail [21]

This famous old cattle trail, running 2000 miles from Texas to Wyoming, was blazed in 1866 by Charles Goodnight and Oliver Loving. In New Mexico, the trail followed the Pecos River north to Fort Sumner, where the government needed beef to feed the Navajos at the Bosque Redondo Reservation.

Lovington [22]

Population—9727   Elevation—3900 ft.

Lovington is named after Robert Florence Love, who founded the town on his homestead in 1908. It was a farming and ranching community until the discovery of the Denton pool after World War II turned it into an oil town. It is the county seat of Lea County.

Flynn-Welch-Yates Oil Well [23]

On April 9, 1924, a well drilled at this site by the partnership of Thomas Flynn, Van Welch, and Martin Yates, Jr. struck oil. It became the first commercial oil well in New Mexico and led to subsequent discoveries of vast amounts of oil and gas. The oil and gas industry has developed into the single greatest source of revenue for the State of New Mexico.

Llano Estacado [24]

Llano Estacado, Stockaded Plain, is southern part of High Plains section, a high plateau of 32,000 square miles in eastern New Mexico and western Texas. Crops are irrigated by "fossil" water pumped from underground sandstones. Deeper are prolific oil and gas pools, the liquid black gold of southeastern New Mexico. Elevation 3,655 feet.

Hobbs [25]

Population—28,794   Elevation—3615 ft.

Named for the family of James Hobbs which homesteaded here in 1907, Hobbs became first a trading village for ranchers and then a major oil town after the discovery of oil by the Midwest Oil Company in 1928.

Llano Estacado [26]

Llano Estacado, Stockaded Plain, is southern part of High Plains section, a high plateau of 32,000 square miles in eastern New Mexico and western Texas. Crops are irrigated by "fossil" water pumped from underground sandstones. Deeper are prolific oil and gas pools, the liquid black gold of southeastern New Mexico. Elevation 3,610 feet.

Oil Country [27]

Southern part of Llano Estacado, Stockaded Plain, overlies prolific oil and gas geologic formations of Pennsylvanian and Permian age; Monument Jal field to west, Drinkard field to south and Elliott Littman to north. At surface, Ogalalla Formation yields gravel and caliche; at depth it supplies precious water. Elevation 3,395 feet.

Carlsbad [28]

Population—25,496   Elevation—3120 ft.

Carlsbad was originally named Eddy after Charles B. Eddy, pioneer cattleman and promoter, but was later re-named for the famous European resort. In 1590 the expedition of Gaspar Castaño de Sosa followed this part of the Pecos River, which in the 19th century had become the center of a vast cattle empire.

Espejo's Trail [29]

Don Antonio de Espejo, leader of the third expedition to explore New Mexico, passed near here on his return to Mexico City in 1583. After learning of the martyrdom of two Franciscan friars from an earlier expedition, he explored the Pueblo country and then followed the Pecos River Valley south.

Loving's Bend [30]

In July 1867, Oliver Loving, a partner in the Goodnight-Loving cattle concern, was seriously wounded in a fight with Comanches. While his companion, "One-Armed" Bill Wilson, went for help, Loving stood off the attack for two days and nights. Loving died from his wounds at Fort Sumner in September.

Carlsbad Caverns National Park [31]

These vast and magnificent caverns contain over 21 miles of explored corridors. The chambers contain countless stalactites and stalagmites unrivaled in size and beauty. The caverns are within a reef that formed in an ancient sea 240 million years ago. Millions of years later, the reef was fractured, allowing ground water to begin work fashioning the caverns.

Guadalupe Mountains [32]

Guadalupe Mountains to southwest rise from Pecos River Valley, with higher southern peaks at 8,750 feet. Bold escarpment is famous Capitán limestone, an ancient reef similar to Great Barrier Reef of Australia, and host to Carlsbad Caverns as well as deep petroleum and underground water. Elevation 3,270 feet.

Artesia [33]

Population—10,385   Elevation—3350 ft.

Artesia, named for the area's many artesian wells, lies on the route of the Pecos Valley cattle trails used by Charles Goodnight, Oliver Loving, and John S. Chisum. The town, established in 1903, is located in what was once part of Chisum's vast cattle empire.

Castaño de Sosa's Route [34]

In 1590-91, Gaspar Castaño de Sosa led an expedition in an unsuccessful attempt to establish a colony in New Mexico. During the winter of 1590, as he pushed north along the Pecos River, the group passed along this route in the vicinity of present-day Artesia and Roswell.

State History of Education Museum [35]

Constructed in 1906, the Lake Arthur Elementary School has been memorialized as the oldest continously used school building in New Mexico. In 1989, the New Mexico legislature designated the structure as the official New Mexico State History of Education Museum. The museum was dedicated on October 12, 1989 and features displays and artifacts from New Mexico's school districts.

Chisum Trail [36]

Sometimes confused with the Chisholm Trail from Texas to Kansas, the Chisum Trail was used by New Mexico rancher John S. Chisum to supply cattle to the Indian agencies in Arizona. In 1875, Chisum sent 11,000 head over this route, which winds from Roswell to Las Cruces, then roughly follows modern I-10 west to Arizona.

High Plains [37]

You are on west edge of High Plains, here sloping eastward to Pecos Valley. Foothills of Capitán Mountains are to northwest and Sierra Blanca to west, an ancient 12,003-foot complex volcano. Canyon of Río Hondo to southwest exposes Permian limestone aquifers that nourish Pecos Valley crops. Elevation 5,100 feet.

Ruidoso [38]

Population—4260   Elevation—6855 ft.

Originally known as Dowlin's Mill, the town was located on the Chisum Trail which ran from the Pecos River to Arizona. By 1885 it had attracted a store, a blacksmith shop, and a post office which was named Ruidoso after the local stream. Several incidents of the Lincoln County War occurred here, including the murder of Paul Dowlin in May 1877.

John H. Tunstall Murder Site [39]

In one of the Lincoln County War's earliest violent encounters, John H. Tunstall was shot and killed at a nearby site on February 18, 1878. Tunstall's death set off a series of violent reprisals between his friends, among whom was William "Billy the Kid" Bonney, and forces of the Murphy/Dolan faction of this tragic conflict. Tunstall, an English businessman, came to New Mexico in 1876.

Blazer's Mill [40]

An early fight in the Lincoln County War occurred near this sawmill on April 5, 1878, when several men of the McSween faction, including Dick Brewer and Billy the Kid, attempted to arrest Buckshot Roberts. Roberts and Brewer were killed, and two others wounded, in the battle that followed.

St. Joseph's Mission [41]

Father Albert Braun, who directed the construction of the remarkable mission church of St. Joseph, served as chaplain in both World Wars. He first came to Mescalero in 1916, and later built this stone church in memory of Americans killed in World War I. It took him almost twenty years to complete, and was dedicated in 1939.

Round Mountain [42]

This cone-shaped landmark about 10 miles from Tularosa was once known as Dead Man's Hill, and has been the backdrop for several military encounters. In April 1868 a small group of soldiers and Tularosa settlers engaged in battle with about 200 Mescalero Apaches.

Mescalero Apache Reservation [43]

The Mescalero Apaches were named for their use of mescal for food. Their economy, based primarily on hunting, gathering and raiding and trading, the Mescaleros occupied much of south-central New Mexico in the 18th and 19th centuries. Since 1871, the Mescaleros have lived on a reservation of about half a million acres, located on part of their ancient homeland.

Tularosa [44]

Population—2536   Elevation—4443 ft.

The first successful European settlement in the Tularosa Basin dates from 1862, when 50 or 60 Hispanic farmers moved from the Río Grande Valley. Heavy Anglo settlement began in the 1880s as settlers and cattlemen from farther east began moving into New Mexico. Tularosa appears as "Oasis" in the novels of western writer Eugene Manlove Rhodes.

Alamogordo [45]

Population—24,024   Elevation—4350 ft.

In 1898 the brothers Charles B. and John A. Eddy, promoters of the El Paso and Northeastern Railroad, laid out and platted a town here. Alamogordo served as a junction with a railroad line to the lumbering operation in the Sacramento Mountains. The first atomic bomb was exploded 60 miles northwest of here on July 16, 1945.

Cloud-Climbing Railroad [46]

In order to provide timber for the construction of his El Paso & Northeastern Railroad north of Alamogordo, Charles B. Eddy in 1898 built a spur into the Sacramento Mountains. The line operated as far as Cloudcroft until 1947. The Cloudcroft Trestle is all that remains.

Dog Canyon [47]
(Cañon del Perro)

For the Mescalero Apaches, Dog Canyon was a favorite camping area and trail through the Sacramento Mountains. It was the scene of several battles in the 19th century. In 1863 a group of Mescaleros was attacked by soldiers, and the survivors were sent to the Bosque Redondo Reservation.

Tularosa Valley [48]

Spectacular escarpment of Sacramento Mountains to east is of Paleozoic sedimentary rocks, well exposed along Dog Canyon. Tularosa Valley is downdropped about 2 miles relative to Sacramentos and San Andrés Mountains on west side of basin. Gypsum dunes of White Sands to west occur only in arid climates. Elevation 4,030 feet.

Pat Garrett Murder Site [49]

Pat Garrett, the Lincoln County Sheriff who shot and killed William "Billy the Kid" Bonney at Fort Sumner in 1881, was himself murdered at a remote site nearby on February 29, 1908. Wayne Brazel, a local cowboy, confessed to shooting Garrett but was acquitted of all charges. The motive and circumstances surrounding Garrett's death are still being debated.

Fort Tularosa [50]

Fort Tularosa was established in 1872 south of present-day Aragon. Two companies of infantry were stationed here to guard the Apaches placed at the Tularosa Southern Apache Reservation. The post was deactivated in 1874 when the Apaches were transferred to another reservation. The fort's garrison was then transferred to Fort Craig, south of Socorro.

Three Rivers [51]

Located in the Tularosa Basin east of the great lava flows known as the malpais, Three Rivers was once prominent in the cattle empires of Albert Bacon Fall, John S. Chisum, and Susie McSween Barber, "the cattle queen of New Mexico." Charles B. Eddy's El Paso & Northeastern Railroad reached here in 1899.

Three Rivers Petroglyphs [52]

Three miles to the east is a mile-long array of pictures pecked into the solid rock walls of a volcanic ridge. They include both geometric and animal forms. They were likely made by prehistoric Mogollón Indians between ca. A.D. 1000 and 1400.

Sierra Blanca [53]

Sierra Blanca, a complex ancient volcano, rises more than 7,300 feet above Tularosa Basin to peak at 12,003 feet. Vertical geologic movement between ranges and basin is about 2 miles. San Andrés Mountains on west side of Tularosa Basin are uplifted on east side and tilted westward. Elevation 4,670 feet.

Carrizozo [54]

Population—1222   Elevation—5438 ft.

Carrizozo, county seat of Lincoln County, was established in 1899, a new town on the El Paso and

Northeastern Railroad. The ghost town of White Oaks, once a booming mining camp, is nearby. Billy the Kid, Sheriff Pat Garrett, Governor Lew Wallace, and Albert Bacon Fall all figured prominently in the history of the area.

Lincoln [55]

Lincoln was the focal point of the notorious Lincoln County War of 1876-79, a complex struggle for political and economic power. Sheriff William Brady, outlaw Billy the Kid, Governor Samuel B. Axtell and cattle baron John S. Chisum were some of the people involved in this violent episode.

Malpais — Valley of Fires [56]

Spanish explorers called this extensive lava flow *malpais,* or badlands. The river of lava that flowed down this "Valley of Fires" erupted from a volcano some 7 miles south of here about 1000 years ago. Extending through the valley for 44 miles, the malpais averages 3 miles in width. This ropy type of lava is called "pahoehoe."

Salinas National Monument [57]

This unique regional complex of prehistoric Indian pueblos and associated 17th-century Franciscan mission ruins constitutes a "capsule in time" in which the first century of Native American-European contact in what is now the United States is preserved. The complex includes Abó, Quarai, and Gran Quivira Ruins. The central visitor center is in Mountainair's historic Shaffer Hotel.

Greathouse Station And Tavern [58]

In late November, 1880, William "Billy the Kid" Bonney, David Rudabaugh and William Wilson were hiding out near here at a store and tavern operated by James Greathouse and a partner named Kuch. The night of November 27, they were surrounded buy a posse. Deputy James Carlyle was accidentally killed when he attempted to negotiate the outlaws' surrender. Bonney and his companions escaped unharmed.

Capitán [59]

Population—762   Elevation—6350 ft.

Many incidents in the Lincoln County War, 1876-79, occurred in the area around Capitán. The promoters Charles B. and John A. Eddy platted the townsite in 1900, after building a spur of the El Paso & Northeastern Railroad from Carrizozo in order to open the Salado coal fields. The mines were abandoned in 1901.

In 1950, a little bear cub, his feet badly burned, was rescued from a forest fire near here. The cub was nursed back to health and flown to Washington, D.C. to become the living symbol of "Smokey Bear" in the U.S. Forest Service's fire prevention program.

Lincoln [60]

Spanish-speaking settlers established a town here in the 1850s, after the U.S. Army began to control the Mescalero Apaches. First known as Las Placitas del Río Bonito, the name of the community was changed to Lincoln when Lincoln County was created in 1869.

Center of the turbulent Lincoln County War, 1876-79, a land and cattle feud marked by violence on both sides. Lincoln's historic landmarks include the Murphy-Dolan store, which later became the Lincoln County Courthouse, the store of John Henry Tunstall, whose murder set off the hostilities, and the house of Alexander McSween, where the final battle was fought.

Fort Stanton [61]
1855-1896

Fort Stanton, named for Captain Henry Stanton, was established to control the Mescalero Apaches. It was burned and evacuated by Union troops in 1861, held briefly by the Confederates, and then reoccupied by Colonel Kit Carson for the Union in 1862. Since its abandonment as a military post, it has been used as a hospital.

OLD LINCOLN COUNTY COURTHOUSE

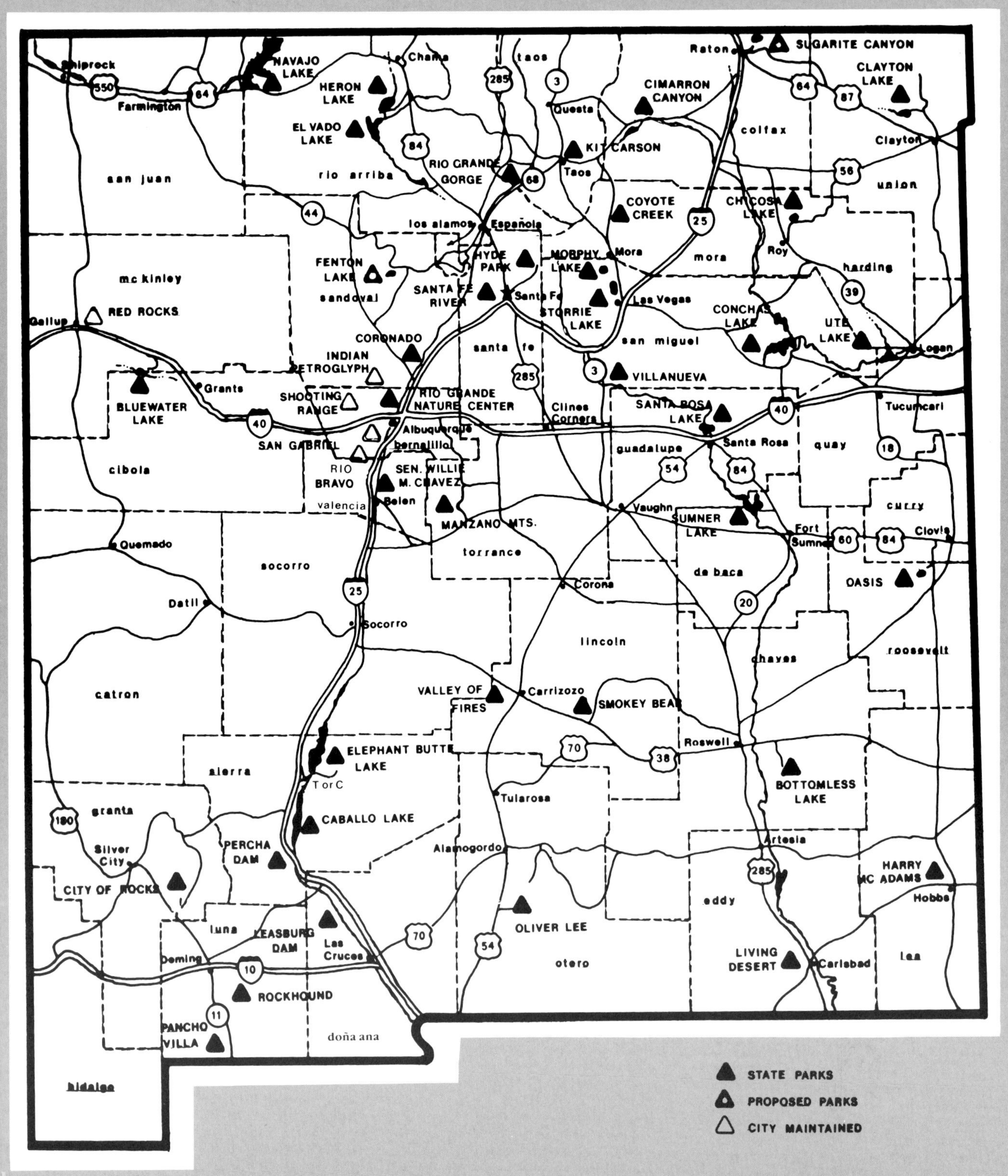

NEW MEXICO STATE PARKS

Bluewater Lake State Park

Rolling hills studded with piñon and juniper trees encircle Bluewater Lake, which provides excellent boating, waterskiing, and fishing. The lake is stocked with rainbow trout and channel catfish, and is the most popular trout fishing lake in the state. Facilities include camping/picnicking sites, and a boat ramp.

Bottomless Lakes State Park

Bordered by high red bluffs, the six small lakes at the park were formed when circulating water dissolved gypsum and salt deposits in underlying rock formations, creating a network of underground cavities. The roofs of some of those caverns collapsed under their own weight, and the resulting sink holes filled with water. Some of the lakes are stocked with trout and swimming is permitted in Lea Lake. There are also hiking trails, visitor center displays, and skin diving opportunities.

Caballo Lake State Park

With the tawny folds of the Caballo Mountains as a backdrop, this park features camping, picnicking, swimming, boating, waterskiing, and fishing. Hiking trails and a playground are also available, along with extensive boating facilities, including a marina. Caballo Lake provides year-round fishing for bass, catfish, and panfish.

Chicosa Lake State Park

This small natural lake was once a watering stop for great herds of cattle that were driven north out of Texas on the Goodnight-Loving Trail. The park's interpretive exhibits . including a chuck wagon and a small herd of longhorn cattle . evoke the life of an earlier, wilder time on New Mexico's vast plains. Chicosa Lake offers fishing as well as camping/picnicking sites.

Cimarron Canyon State Park

This high mountain park is part of a state wildlife area and is managed by the New Mexico State Park Division in cooperation with the New Mexico Department of Game and Fish. Trout fishing is excellent in the Cimarron River, and the park offers fine opportunities for backcountry hiking and wildlife viewing. The crenellated rock formation known as the Palisades is popular with rock climbers.

City of Rocks State Park

Wind and water gradually sculpted the volcanic tuff at City of Rocks, creating the rows of monolithic blocks that gave this park its name. Camping/picnicking sites are tucked away among these Stonehenge-like volcanic formations, and the park also features a cactus garden, hiking trails, and a playground.

Clayton Lake State Park

The rolling grasslands around Clayton Lake were once a domain of the huge buffalo herds that ranged the Great Plains. Many years prior to this, dinosaurs ruled the area, as indicated by a series of tracks embedded in the rock near the lake. Clayton Lake is stocked with rainbow trout and channel catfish, and also provides good bass and walleye fishing. The lake serves as a wintering area for waterfowl.

Conchas Lake State Park

This 25-mile long reservoir offers a full spectrum of water-based activities—boating, waterskiing, fishing—along with two modern marinas. The lake has some of the best walleye and crappie fishing in the state. As a resort facility, Conchas provides recreation for all seasons, including waterfowl hunting in winter. There are also camping/picnicking areas and a nine-hole golf course.

Coronado State Park

With splendid views of the Sandía Mountains and the Río Grande, the park offers camping/picnicking sites adjacent to Coronado State Monument, site of the prehistoric Indian pueblo of Kuaua. The monument offers a museum with exhibits about the history of the pueblo and an interpretive trail through the ruins.

Coyote Creek State Park

Secluded in the foothills of the Sangre de Cristo Mountains beside a stream dotted with beaver ponds, this park offers hiking, camping/picnicking sites, and fishing for rainbow and brown trout.

El Vado Lake State Park

This mountain reservoir offers boating, waterskiing, and fishing, as well as excellent hiking on the scenic hiking trail connecting El Vado and Heron lakes. Ice fishing is a popular winter sport here, and trout and salmon are caught year-round.

Elephant Butte Lake State Park

Situated beside the huge, 36,000-acre Elephant Butte Reservoir, this is one of the largest and most popular parks in New Mexico. It combines boating, waterskiing, fishing, and other water-based sports with land activities such as camping, picnicking, and hiking. Fish caught year-round at Elephant Butte Lake include various species of bass, channel catfish, and crappie.

Fenton Lake State Park

Surrounded by imposing mountains and beautiful ponderosa pine woodlands, Fenton Lake has long been a popular fishing and camping retreat. This area offers both lake and stream fishing for rainbow trout, and many deer, turkey, and elk inhabit the immediate vicinity. The park area is also used for winter sports such as cross-country skiing and dogsled racing.

Heron Lake State Park

Set in a region of tall ponderosa pine trees, Heron Reservoir has been designated a "quiet lake," where motorboats may operate at no more than trolling speed. The lake provides excellent sailing as well as fine trout and salmon fishing. Facilities at Heron Lake include a visitor center with interpretive displays, camping/picnicking sites, hiking trails, and boat ramps.

Hyde Memorial State Park

Perched at an elevation of 8,300 feet in the Sangre de Cristo Mountains near the Santa Fe Ski Basin, Hyde Park is used as a basecamp for backpackers and skiers venturing into the Santa Fe National Forest. The park includes a skating pond and a sledding area for winter use, a playground, and camping/picnicking, and recreational vehicle sites.

Kit Carson Memorial State Park

The graves of famed frontiersman Kit Carson and his family, as well as those of several other notable historic figures, are found in the Kit Carson Cemetery within the park. Park facilities include picnic areas, a bicycling/walking path, tennis courts, a playground, and a basketball court that doubles as a skating pond in winter.

Leasburg Dam State Park

Built in 1908, the historic Leasburg Diversion Dam channels water from the Río Grande to irrigate the vast farming area of the Upper Mesilla Valley. The dam also provides a pleasant spot for fishing, and canoes and kayaks may be used on the river. Picnicking and camping facilities are also available.

Living Desert State Park

Dedicated to interpretation of the Chihuahuan Desert, this park is an indoor/outdoor museum of New Mexico plants and animals. Exhibits concerning natural history and environmental themes include a desert arboretum with extensive cactus gardens, an aviary, and a nocturnal exhibit. Over 60 animal species and 1,000 plant species are on view at Living Desert.

Manzano Mountains State Park

Nestled in the heavily timbered foothills of the Manzano Mountains, this park features hiking, camping, and picnicking. It is an excellent place for bird-watching.

Harry McAdams State Park

This intensively landscaped park offers cool greenery surrounding a pair of small ponds. Facilities include picnicking, recreational vehicle camping sites, a playground, sports fields, and a visitor center with historical exhibits about the Llano Estacado and Hobbs region.

Navajo Lake State Park/Pine River

Centered on a lake of 13,000 surface acres, the park offers camping/picnicking areas, a visitor center with extensive interpretive displays, and a boat ramp. Boating and waterskiing are popular here, and the lake provides good fishing for trout, salmon, bass, catfish, and crappie. Trout fishing on the San Juan River is exceptional.

Navajo Lake State Park/Sims Mesa

Located on the southeast side of Navajo Lake, the secluded Sims Mesa site offers campsites, a boat ramp, and a marina.

Oasis State Park

In this desert setting, a homesteader in 1902 planted the trees of what has become a true oasis. The park offers a small fishing pond stocked with rainbow trout, picnicking facilities, and an attractive campground set among towering cottonwoods and shifting sand dunes.

Oliver Lee Memorial State Park

Named for a pioneer New Mexico rancher, this park is set against the steep, west-facing escarpment of the Sacramento Mountains on the edge of the Tularosa Basin. Located at the mouth of Dog Canyon, where springs and seeps support a variety of rare and endangered plant species, this site has drawn human visitors for thousands of years. The park offers picnicking and camping facilities, hiking trails, and extensive visitor center displays.

Pancho Villa State Park

Pancho Villa State Park commemorates the historic Columbus Raid of 1916. Ruins of Camp Furlong, headquarters for General John Pershing's expeditionary force, still exist at the park. The old Columbus Customs Service building has been restored to house exhibits about the raid and Pershing's Punitive Expedition into Mexico in pursuit of Pancho Villa and his raiders. Camping/picnicking sites are scattered throughout a beautiful desert botanical garden.

Percha Dam State Park

Set in the deep shade of towering cottonwood trees, this park features fishing near a historic dam that diverts river water for irrigation. There are camping/picnicking sites, hiking trails, and excellent bird-watching opportunities.

Red Rock State Park

Located at the foot of massive red sandstone buttes, this park offers modern campgrounds and picnicking areas. Red Rock is the site of the Gallup Inter-Tribal Indian Ceremonial held annually in August, and the park's facilities include a large arena for rodeos, an auditorium/convention center, and historical exhibits.

Río Grande Gorge State Park

With spectacular views and some of the finest public fishing in New Mexico, this park runs along the banks of the Río Grande. From the Colorado border through the park, the "great river" offers exciting white-water boating through a deep canyon. There are four major camping/picnicking areas along the river.

Rockhound State Park

Located on the rugged slopes of the Florida Mountains, this is one of the most unusual parks in the nation. Here "rockhounds" are encouraged to take home samples of rocks and minerals. The park also offers camping and picnicking facilities, hiking trails, and a playground.

Santa Fe River State Park

The pleasant, tree-lined walkways and shaded picnic benches of this small park flank the Santa Fe River as it meanders through the heart of the oldest capital city in the United States. Pioneer traders and trail drivers brought their wagons to a halt along the river at the end of their long, arduous journey on the Santa Fe Trail.

Santa Rosa Lake State Park

Pronghorn antelope may be seen grazing near this reservoir on the Pecos River, at the edge of the Llano Estacado – the famed "Stockaded Plains." The park offers water sports; fishing for catfish, bass, and walleyes; camping/picnicking sites, a visitor center, and a boat ramp.

Smokey Bear Historical State Park

This park commemorates Smokey Bear, and describes the history and development of this national symbol of forest fire prevention. The original Smokey is buried here within sight of the mountain where he was found, orphaned by a fire raging in the Lincoln National Forest. The park offers extensive historical exhibits, as well as a trail that identifies native plants.

Storrie Lake State Park

Long a popular spot for rainbow trout fishing, Storrie Lake also features boating, swimming, and waterskiing. Facilities include camping/picnicking sites, a boat ramp, a playground, and a visitor information center.

Sugarite Canyon State Park

This heavily wooded mountainous park, located on the Colorado-New Mexico border, was formerly the site of a thriving coal camp. There are two fishing lakes in the New Mexico portion of the canyon, and another lake lies just across the border in Colorado. Wild turkey and deer are plentiful in the park vicinity, and facilities include hiking trails and camping/picnicking sites. The colorful history of the canyon and region is described in the visitor center.

Sumner Lake State Park

Sumner Reservoir offers boating, waterskiing, and fishing, as well as camping and other outdoor recreational opportunities. The lake is stocked with walleyes, bass, channel catfish, and crappie.

Ute Lake

Offering the best walleye fishing in New Mexico, this reservoir on the Canadian River also provides good fishing for both white and largemouth bass, channel catfish, and crappie. Park facilities include camping/picnicking sites, a playground, boat ramps, and a marina.

Valley of Fires State Park

Valley of Fires is situated amid the black, fissured volcanic rock of a malpais lava flow, which is one of the youngest and best-preserved lava fields in the United States. The park features an interpretive nature trail that identifies some of the plants and animals native to the malpais. Camping and picnicking sites are also available.

Villanueva

Couched between high red sandstone bluffs in a beautiful valley of the Pecos River, this park is located near the picturesque Spanish colonial village of Villanueva. The park offers hiking trails with historical markers, and camping/picnicking sites.

PANCHO VILLA . CIRCA 1914

Other New Mexico State Parks:
Shooting Range State Park
Río Grande Nature Center State Park
Sen. Willie M. Chávez State Park
Indian Petroglyph State Park
Río Bravo State Park
San Gabriel State Park

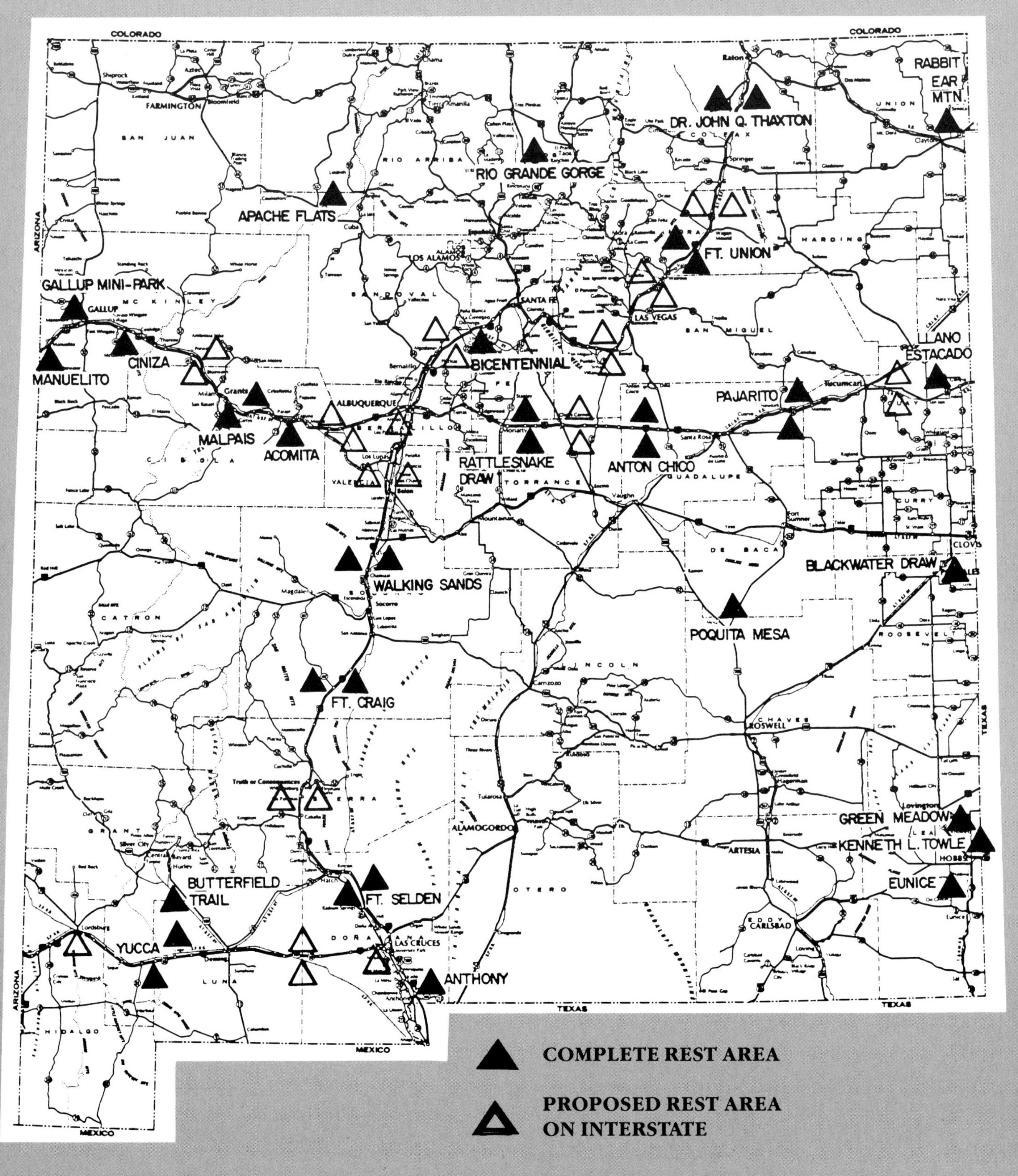

NEW MEXICO SAFETY REST AREAS

ACOMITA REST AREA

LA BAJADA REST AREA

A few decades ago, the first highway rest or roadside rest areas in New Mexico consisted of little more than pull-off spots along the side of the highway where motorists could relax, repair the car, or have a picnic. The present safety rest area system has changed a great deal from the early waysides. Its overall purpose . . . that of providing a haven for the driver and passengers seeking rest from the monotony and fatigue of driving and travel . . . is still of prime importance.

New Mexico's rest areas which have been built since 1965 contain not only modern restrooms, water facilities, sanitary stations for RV'ers, lighted parking, and picnic facilities, but may also feature telephones where possible and horse corrals for unloading and resting horses in transit. Sites for these rest areas have been selected for scenic value, availability of utilities, and approach visibility. Architectural design for the structures has been specifically selected for each area to portray some significant feature of the general locale or to blend into the scenic quality of the site.

Examples of two architectural designs are shown on this page. One, Acomita, incorporates the use of native stone and replicates native residences in the near vicinity. Further, the site is a flat stone mesa typical of the area. The other picture is of a territorial style building typical of the melding of Spanish, adobe and colonial styles in and around the Santa Fe Trail.

ALPHABETICAL INDEX